How

Completely Cool

Kathryn Lamb

Piccadilly Press • London

Kathryn Lamb lives 'quietly' in Gillingham, Dorset, with her husband, Adrian Bovey, and their six children and numerous animals. Adrian has three teenage children.

Without the help of all these people (not so much the animals) she would have found it a lot more difficult to write this book. She would like to thank them all, including some very special grandparents.

Kathryn draws cartoons for *Private Eye* and *The Oldie*. She has illustrated a number of books for Piccadilly Press including: *For Weddings, A Funeral and When You Can't Flush The Loo; You're My Best Friend – I Hate You; A Right Royal History; The Good, The Bad and The Ghastly: World War II* and *The Good, The Bad and The Ghastly: The Wild West*.

She is also the author of the extremely well-reviewed *Help!* series. *Help! My Family is Driving me Crazy!* was selected by *The Bookseller* as one of a hundred best books for Spring 1997: '. . . *it hits just the right humorous note.*'

Other books by Kathryn Lamb,
published by Piccadilly Press:

HELP! MY FAMILY IS DRIVING ME CRAZY!
HELP! MY SOCIAL LIFE IS A MESS!
HELP! LET ME OUT OF HERE!
BOYWATCHING!
GIRLS ARE FROM SATURN, BOYS ARE FROM JUPITER

CONTENTS

For Charlotte Louise
and Isobel Christina Bovey

CHAPTER 1

Do YOU Need This Book?

Tick any of the following statements which apply to you, or you agree with:

❑ Going round the supermarket with Mum is fun.

❑ If I want to look really smart, I usually borrow Mum's/Dad's clothes, or allow them to advise me. They have excellent taste, and I value their opinions.

❑ It is important to have a cheery smile on your face at all times, in order to brighten other people's lives.

❑ My favourite song is called, 'I'd like to teach the world to sing'.

❑ I make a point of sitting near to the teachers at school, so I can give my full attention to what they are saying.

❑ I start my homework as soon as I get home. In fact, I have placed my desk as near to the front door as possible, so that I can immediately sit down and get on with it.
❑ I have asked my parents to get rid of the television, as it is an unnecessary distraction.
❑ I eat plenty of vegetables (mostly raw) and fibre-rich foods, since Mummy tells me this will help with my 'little problem'. I eat a good breakfast, which includes a cereal called Sensible.

If you ticked any of the above statements, YOU NEED THIS BOOK. If you didn't tick anything, the chances are that you are a cool dude already. So you're just reading this book for a laugh, while gliding along on your skateboard, listening to your Walkman (mind that lamppost) . . .

REMEMBER: It is only human to lose your cool from time to time, and the occasional (or more frequent) uncool episodes and incidents in your life unite you with the majority of human beings.

COOL QUIZ

But how do you get out of a situation which has become too uncool to handle? What is your Cool Quota? (CQ) Answer the questions in the following quiz to find out!

1 Your mum brings out an embarrassing photo of you as a baby on a rug with no clothes on, and shows it to your friends. What do you say?

A 'Mum! HOW COULD YOU?! THAT'S SO EMBARRASSING!' And you stamp your foot, or plonk yourself down on the sofa with arms folded and a face like thunder.

B 'Oh, wasn't I just SOOOO adorable! Isn't that the cutest thing?'

C 'That's not me. That's Paul. I know it's a bit difficult to tell, because the rug's in the way. But you can still see it's Paul. Never mind, Mum – I've heard that memory is one of the first things to go . . .'

2 Your dad insists on performing a magic trick in front of your friends, but it goes hopelessly wrong. How do you react?

YOU STAND IN THE DOORWAY, CRINGING VISIBLY...

A You stand in the doorway, cringing visibly, rigid with embarrassment, unable to move or speak, blushing horribly, and sweating profusely.

B You shriek; 'Oh, isn't my dad just so adorable? Don't you just want to give him a great big hug?' You proceed to do so.

C You say; 'Don't worry, Dad – it's cool. Come on, guys – let's go and watch TV.'

3 Person-U-Like chats you up for the very first time. How do you react?

A You are stricken dumb. Your jaw sags slightly, and you gaze at him/her, open-mouthed. Eventually, you manage to say 'Guurghh . . .'

B You exclaim; 'Wow! Do you fancy me? I've fancied you for ages! Shall we go out together? How many children do you want?'

C You say, 'Hi!' and give a little smile, before wandering off to get yourself a drink, or something to eat.

4 Your mum insists you wear a naff, yuk-brown raincoat before she will let you go out with your friends, who are waiting at the door. What do you do?

A Throw a fit, stamp your foot, shout at your mum 'It's HORRIBLE! So are you!' and stomp off to your room, slamming the door shut behind you, leaving everyone not knowing quite what to do or say next, and leaving your friends getting wet, waiting for you in the rain. (The final straw is when one of them asks your mum if THEY can borrow the raincoat . . .)

B Make a great show of putting the raincoat on and parading around in it, striking poses and attitudes, and generally playing the fool.

C You turn the situation to your advantage by shouting 'Thanks, Mum!', seizing the raincoat and dashing to your room with it. You return a few minutes later

PLAYING THE FOOL IS FUN — BUT UNCOOL

wearing the raincoat, buttoned up to the neck. Your friends look at you a bit strangely, until you have turned the corner. You then rip off the wretched raincoat, revealing that you have used it to conceal the fact that you are wearing THAT sexy mini-dress/THAT T-shirt with the parent-offending slogan which your mum has FORBIDDEN you to wear in public . . .

5 You are with a crowd which includes Person-U-Like. You are all chilling out in someone's room, listening to music. The CD comes to an end, and you bend down to take it out of the machine when, to your complete horror, you fart – audibly (there is no polite way of putting this. Sorry). It is the single most desperately UNCOOL thing you have EVER done in your life. How can you possibly ever recover?

A You run out of the room, out of the house, all the way back to your own room, where you intend to hide for the rest of your life.

B One or more of your friends is almost bound to start laughing. You join in the laughter until you are rolling around the floor, shrieking hysterically.

C You say, calmly; 'Whoops! Too many beans!' or, 'Mum's chilli is something else – you don't want to know the effect it has on the dog!' You then put on your favourite music, and close your eyes for a while, in order to enjoy it more.

6 Your parents are refusing to let you go to Gary Coolford's party, since they have heard rumours that his parties tend to get rather wild. How do you deal with this?

A You shout at your parents, 'I HATE you! Are you completely determined to RUIN my whole life?!' Then you storm off to your room, slamming the door (again), and rip up a photo of your mum and dad into tiny shreds which you throw on the floor and jump up and down on.

B You have a bright idea. 'I know! Why don't you come with me, Mum? You could come too, Dad! I'm sure Gary wouldn't mind. We'd all have a great time!'

C You pause to consider your parents' point of view, and reason with yourself that in a few years' time you should have a place of your own, and then you can do what you like. In the meantime, you say, 'I know it's hard for you, Mum and Dad. You get worried because you care, I guess. But I wouldn't do anything stupid. Anyway, I'll accept what you say, because I'm still under your roof. If you don't want me to go to Gary's party, that's cool. But if you change your minds and decide to let me go, that's cool, too.' Your parents are so stunned and taken aback by this sudden outburst of maturity and downright coolness, that they decide to let you go to Gary's party, after all.

MOSTLY A'S: Your CQ (Cool Quota) is a little on the low side. You NEED this book, but there is certainly hope for you. Try to RELAX. Remember that running away is effective but *not* cool. Remember too that no one has ever (to my knowledge) actually died of embarrassment. And perhaps things (or parents) are not quite as embarrassing or dreadful as you think they are.

MOSTLY B'S: You have obviously read a book called *How to Be Seriously Uncool* and taken its advice to heart. It's probably time to CHANGE, for your own sake (and everyone else's).

LOW CQ

MOSTLY C'S: Wow! You are some kind of Cool Dude, man! Yo! Your CQ is right off the top of the scale! You may not need this book – but why not read it anyway? You like to do things for a laugh (but never an over-loud or forced laugh – in fact, a cool smile is more your style). You may even pick up some new tips to add to your repertoire.

HIGH CQ
(COOL QUOTA)

WHAT IS COOL?

Cool is . . . knowing what to say. Cool is . . . being confident. Cool is . . . looking good. Cool is . . . knowing you're looking good. Cool is . . . being in control. Cool is . . . FOCUSED. But perhaps cool is more than that. Cool is . . . not getting stressed if you *don't* always know exactly what to say. Cool is . . . not caring too much if you're not always in complete control (who is?). Cool is . . . being relaxed and laid-back about life in general. Cool should be . . . FUN.

COOL HAT

COOL HAT

UNCOOL HAT

The word COOL may mean different things to different people. You may not consider it cool to wear a floppy velvet hat which comes down over your face so you have to hold your head right up and peer down your nose to see where you're going. But Laura Pemberton wears hers all the time, AND she looks good in it. Perhaps being cool is a matter of not being afraid to be an individual. You strut your funky stuff in your own way. On the other hand, it is difficult to strut your funky stuff in an anorak, a bobble hat and a pair of cast-off slacks (mega uncool name for trousers/strides, etc.) of your dad's, which your mum has taken up so that they are too short for you. So – there must be certain things which are generally (if not universally) recognised as being UNCOOL, just as there are things which are definitely COOL.

IT IS DIFFICULT TO STRUT YOUR FUNKY STUFF IN A BOBBLE HAT AND ANORAK ...

The *Concise Oxford Dictionary* defines 'cool' as 'unexcited, calm', as in 'cool and collected'. So you could just as easily say to someone, 'Wow! You're looking really collected!' But, for some reason, it was the word 'cool' which caught on. The dictionary also mentions that 'cool' is just another word for 'excellent'. As far as I'm concerned, the *Concise Oxford Dictionary* is an excellent book, but there is nothing particularly cool about it, so I am going to put it back on the shelf.

Misleading phrases involving the word 'cool':

✦ 'As cool as a cucumber.' Let's face it – there is nothing particularly cool about a long green vegetable which your dad/ grandad grows in the garden. It is even less cool if your name is Jeremy Witherspoon, and your mum makes dinky little triangular, cucumber sandwiches with the crusts removed, and sends you to school with them.

AS COOL AS A CUCUMBER

AS GROOVY AS A GHERKIN

✦ 'Cool hands, warm heart.' Just because you have poor circulation, and your hands are like frozen bunches of carrots (different colour, hopefully), doesn't necessarily mean that you are going to give away all your money (what money?) to charity at the earliest opportunity. What are 'cool hands' anyway? Perhaps, if you are a girl, they are beautifully manicured, with long, slender fingers and perfectly varnished nails (real ones, not bitten. It is uncool to bite your nails, and even less cool to put on false ones, and then

AS COMATOSE AS A CUCUMBER

bite THOSE). If you are a boy, hands can sometimes seem quite uncool things, flapping about at the end of your arms. The coolest thing to do with them seems to be to put them in your pockets, but people (such as teachers) keep shouting at you to take them out again. Your mum or dad doesn't help: 'Stop fiddling with that yo-yo/bunch of keys/piece of string! Don't you have anything better to do? Go and get on with your homework!'

RULES OF COOL

FIRST RULE OF COOL

Don't worry about it. RELAX.

Let's summarise. Cool is calm, cool is collected (as in 'a collected hat', etc.) or 'together', cool is being relaxed and unfazed by events without actually becoming comatose ('as comatose as a cucumber'). You can cultivate a cool exterior, if you wish (wear your cool shades to disguise the fact that you are crying your eyes out during a soppy film). You don't have to know exactly what to say ALL the time. Try saying nothing, so that you seem as if you KNOW what's going on, but you don't really need to comment (there is a saying, 'Silence is cool'. Or was it 'golden'? Does it matter?). Of course, it's fine if you DO know exactly what to say ALL the time, in every single situation that life throws at you. This is known as being

Supercool. Other people will probably admire you for your cool and perfect poise, but they may be slightly intimidated by it (how *do* you do it?). There is something a little unreal about being *so* in control. Most ordinary mortals feel vaguely reassured when they see a Supercool Dude faced with a situation where they lose it ever so slightly . . .

As in other areas of life, being COOL is a question of getting the balance right. It isn't cool to trip over your own feet, even if they are an uncool size fifteen, and fall flat on your face at the perfectly-formed feet of Person-U-Like – but it *is* human . . .

SECOND RULE OF COOL

Don't try too hard to impress. You don't need to put on an act. People should take you as you are, and like you for yourself. If there are one or two people who don't seem to like you, don't bother with them. You don't need them (they may come round in the end, anyway. Or they may not. It doesn't matter).

There is another saying, 'You can't please all the people all of the time.' No, of course you can't. And if you are going to be truly cool, you should avoid *trying* to please.

NOTE: It is cool to have seen the film or heard the album that everyone is talking about. But if you haven't, it is better to keep quiet (Quiet is Cool) rather than show off and say, 'I thought Harrison Hunk was amazing,' only for someone to say, 'Harrison Hunk wasn't in it.' If you can't easily get to see the film or hear the album, try to read a review in a newspaper/magazine, so that you know what people are talking about.

REMEMBER: Being cool does NOT mean being perfect. Consider the following: 'I temper all my success with a decent amount of failure.' This is a cool quote from a cool OLD guy, called Suggs (it is ultra cool to have just *one* name). There are one or two Cool Old Farts around. Lenny Henry is one of them. The leaders of New Cool

GIRLS' FEET CAN BE COOL

BOYS' FEET ARE USUALLY CONSIDERED UNCOOL

are, among others: Leonardo, Michael Owen, Uma Thurman, Cameron Diaz, the babe in Year twelve whom you can't take your eyes off, the hunky bloke who ignores you in the hall as you switch classes . . .

AND WHY IT DOESN'T ALWAYS WORK

UNFAIR SITUATION NO. 1
THE COOL SCENE

Suni Lal is in his room, getting ready to go to a party. He is dancing (COOL dancing) to his favourite CD, and feels supercool and confident. His new, spotlessly white shirt seems to glow with an almost unearthly radiance in the subdued lighting of his room. He practises his slow smile, with a slight, humorous twitching of the lips, which he is certain will have girls falling at his feet. He runs his hands through his hair, which is silky, shining . . . He smells WONDERFUL (half a can of COOL, the great new twenty-four hour deodorant), and he is ready to PARTY . . .

THE UNCOOL SCENE

Suni Lal arrives at the party. Someone has forgotten to turn down the lights, and his white shirt is completely drowned out by the bright, overhead lights. He notices a beautiful babe waving in his direction. He smiles his special smile . . . only to realise that the beautiful babe

(Babe-U-Like) is waving at someone just behind him. He turns, and sees that the guy (Guy-U-Don't-Like) she is waving to is wearing an uncool greenish jumper (possibly hand-knitted by a doting mother or granny), which he takes off to reveal an even *less* cool, shapeless, faded T-shirt and that he has hair like a loo-brush (or perhaps it is a small dog or guinea-pig sitting on top of his head), and a very pronounced Adam's apple which wobbles up and down his throat. Suni watches with a kind of horrified fascination as Beautiful Babe and Loo-Brush Man HUG EACH OTHER.

Suni tries to enjoy himself, but his cool seems to have deserted him. He finds that he has developed a high-pitched giggle, which he is sure he never had before. His lips twitch nervously, rather than sexily.

BEAUTIFUL BABE AND LOO-BRUSH MAN

He returns home early, and slumps in an armchair, looking depressed. Mrs Lal asks him what the matter is.

'It's nothing, Mum. I just lost my cool.'

'Did you, dear? I'm sure it can't be far away. Have you looked under the bed?'

THIRD RULE OF COOL

It is necessary to accept that a sad consequence of 'cool' is that you are almost bound to lose it occasionally. Just when you need it most, it deserts you. Such is life. Remember the First Rule of Cool (don't worry about it – relax), and your COOL will come back. As you get more used to the embarrassing/awkward situations which life seems determined to throw you into, you are more likely to succeed in keeping your cool.

AND WHY IT DOESN'T ALWAYS WORK

SITUATION NO.1

You can be wearing your coolest hat and your most together pair of trousers, and Person-U-Like will STILL fail to notice you exist. Instead, they walk off with someone you consider completely UNCOOL. *WHY?* No one can answer this question satisfactorily. It is UNFAIR. But it happens.

What do do you do about it?

Don't let it get to you. There are plenty more fish/babes in the sea. There was a song called, 'I'm going to wash

that man right out of my hair' (or it could be a boy or girl). You could try this.

SITUATION NO. 2

THE COOL SCENE

Laura Pemberton is at a party. She is wearing her cool hat, but is feeling a little hot in it. The room is crowded and airless. Her date is busy chatting with his mates and she is getting tired of waiting for him to talk to *her*. She gets up suddenly (*too* suddenly), and everything goes black (or it may just be because the hat is over her eyes). She faints. Her date is at her side instantly, asking if she is OK. People rush to throw open windows, and someone fetches her a drink of water. Laura feels better, and enjoys the attention. Her date stays with her for the rest of the evening.

THE UNCOOL SCENE

Suni Lal is at the same party. He has no girlfriend, and he is bored. He observes how Laura's date (and a large number of other people) rush to her side when she faints. He wonders if the same thing would work for HIM (would a beautiful girl rush to his side and cradle his head in her lap?). He decides to give it a go . . . Unfortunately, he falls heavily, with a loud thump, and bangs his head on the edge of a table (whereas Laura subsided gently and

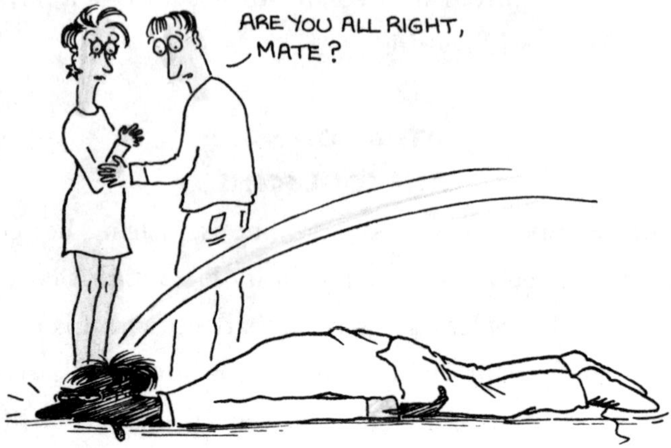

gracefully into a semi-sitting position). Laura's date, who is standing nearby, asks, 'Are you all right, mate?'

'Yeah, I'm fine,' says Suni, getting back on his feet.

'Do you want me to call your folks, or something, and get someone to come and take you home?'

'No! No, honestly. I'm fine. Never been better.'

Suni notices that quite a lot of girls are staring at him, but none of them seems particularly inclined to cradle his head in her lap. It is disappointing. It is also unfair.

SAD BUT TRUE – COOL FOR BOYS/COOL FOR GIRLS

There is more pressure on boys to be Cool Dudes. They are expected (not necessarily by YOU, but by the world at large) to be strong and fairly unemotional.

COOL FOR GIRLS (AND NOT FOR BOYS)

✦ It is cool for girls to cry occasionally (although not continuously). People are usually sympathetic, and will put their arms around the Weeping One. An exception to this rule is the Supercool Guy who objects to girls weeping all over him and getting the shoulder of his best shirt wet.

It is not cool for boys to break down and cry, except on rare occasions. People react differently when a girl cries to the way they do when a boy cries.

WHEN A GIRL CRIES . . .

Girl: I can't handle it any more! It's all too much! BOO HOO!

Parent: Come here, love! Tell me all about it! Here's a tissue . . .

Best Friend: Go on – let it all out. I'm here for you.

WHEN A BOY CRIES . . .

Boy: I can't handle it any more! It's all too much! BOO HOO!

Parent: Well, crying won't help. Go outside and get some fresh air. Come back when you're feeling better.

Best Mate: Oh . . . god. Please . . . PLEASE . . . don't do . . . THAT! Er, I mean, I don't know what to say. Things could be worse, you know. You might be dead! Ha ha! Oh, please stop crying! Someone might see . . .

✦ It is cool for girls to do body-building and weight-training, and even to play rugby (if they wish to). But it is very uncool indeed for a boy if he is struggling to lift something heavy, and a girl comes along and does it for him.

✦ It is cool for girls to wear trousers. It is NOT cool for boys to wear skirts/dresses.

COOL FOR BOYS (AND NOT FOR GIRLS)

✦ It is cool for boys to sit or sprawl in any position they like (mainly because they are not wearing skirts or dresses). It is not cool for a girl to hitch up her skirt and sprawl over the nearest sofa, with one foot up on the back rest and the other on the floor. This sort of behaviour would cause embarrassment to some boys, and attract leering glances and sniggering from others, which most girls can do without. But boys can throw themselves into the most abandoned and relaxing positions they like, and no one minds.

RELAXED. UNCOOL.

✦ There is more pressure on girls to wear something new/short/tight, or to enhance or improve their looks with make-up, etc. This is usually fun if you have the time and money to spend on make-up, etc, but it can be a hassle if you are in a hurry and you manage to smudge mascara all

RELAXED. COOL.

over your nose and smear lipstick all the way from mouth to ear. A boy can arrive at a party wearing no make-up, having not brushed his hair for three days, and still look COOL. If a girl arrives at a party having not brushed her hair for three days, the chances are that she looks A MESS.

BOY ARRIVING AT PARTY, HAVING NOT BRUSHED HAIR FOR THREE DAYS, LOOKS COOL...

GIRL ARRIVING AT PARTY, HAVING NOT BRUSHED HAIR FOR THREE DAYS, LOOKS A MESS...

CHAPTER 2

The Uncoolest Cut Of All – Parents!

Your parents have devoted a lot of time and put a lot of effort from your very earliest years into bringing you up to be . . . UNCOOL. They have not done this deliberately (well, probably not), but there is always the temptation to bring you up to be like themselves (uncool).

Of course, there ARE parents who are COOL. But they are not YOUR parents.

THE ENDLESS LIST OF WHAT PARENTS DO TO TOTALLY EMBARRASS YOU

✦ They decide to name you after the place where you were conceived. This is fine if you were conceived on the island of Bali (Bali is a cool name), but not so good if you were conceived in Wolverhampton.

PARENTS – WHO'D HAVE THEM?
(THE UNCOOLEST CUT OF ALL...)

✦ They call you Twurpin (from *Ye Ancient Booke of Mystical Names*) or Starburst (arguably a cool name way back in the Sixties or Seventies, but now a kind of chewy sweet). Didn't it occur to them that Starburst Miller-Thorpington is a bit of a mouthful?

✦ They get all soppy, and give you a big hug in front of your friends, calling you by a silly pet name, invented when you were a baby. If your friends know you as Jez or Tamara, it will ruin your image completely if they find out you have a name like Whoopsie-Pops or Jub-Jub.

WARNING TO PARENTS :
AVOID CALLING YOUR OFFSPRING NAMES LIKE 'PRECIOUS' OR 'SAUSAGE' IN FRONT OF THEIR FRIENDS ...

✦ If you are a boy, your mum may give you a big kiss on the cheek in front of your mates, leaving a lipstick mark (she may go on to make this worse by attempting to rub it off with a handkerchief). She may also ruffle your hair (you prefer to ruffle it yourself, and do not need her help).

COMBATTING PARENTAL EMBARRASSMENT

1 THE SILLY NAME

✦ If your parents have given you a stupid name, you can always change it. Instead of Cedric or Prudence, you can tell people your name is Zane or Skye. Unfortunately, of course, teachers at school are inclined to give the game away: 'Is Prudence Pilkington in school today?' (No – not if she can help it.)

✦ As mentioned before, it is ultra-cool to have just ONE name (such as Sting, Bono, Lightning). It is necessary to choose the name carefully, however. You are unlikely to succeed if you call yourself Flump, for instance: 'And here to sing her fab new single is . . . er . . . Flump . . .'

✦ Be thankful that you are not (or perhaps you are) the offspring of the sort of American parent who calls their son Hank Z Z Z Zimmermeyer III, or their daughter

Angelbaby Moosedroppings-Loveheart. It is reassuring to think that there is usually some poor dude who is worse off than you.

2 THEIR PRESENCE

Parents should avoid behaving in a way likely to cause severe and lasting damage to their offspring's Cool. They can avoid doing this very effectively by the simple expedient of not being there. They should remember the saying, 'Parents should be *not* heard and *not* seen.' They should make sure the fridge is well-stocked, and then bow out gracefully. When their offspring arrives home with friends, they should retire immediately to the airing cupboard, or to the bottom of the garden (a shed is useful if it is raining), or disappear behind a newspaper, leaving the way clear for the offspring to maintain their Cool/Street Cred.

THE COOL SCENE

Laura Pemberton arrives home after school with three of her friends (Fran, Jo and Pippi). They check out all the cool parts of the house: TV, video, hi-fi system, computer, fridge, cat, Laura's own room. Then they chill out in the living-room, and watch TV. Things are going really well. Laura's parents have thoughtfully gone OUT. Unfortunately, they decide to ruin everything by coming back. They even have the audacity to bring Laura's little brother with them (*couldn't* they have left him behind somewhere?).

THE UNCOOL SCENE

MR PEMBERTON *(Dad)*: Well, I don't think I've had the pleasure of meeting these lovely ladies before!

(Laura's friends look nervously over their shoulders before they realise that Laura's dad is talking to THEM.)

MR PEMBERTON: Introduce me then, Laura. Laura!

LAURA: Er, yes, Dad. This is Fran – Jo – Pippi.

MR PEMBERTON: And I'm Laura's dad! (*This is a statement of the glaringly and embarrassingly obvious.*)

MR PEMBERTON (*carrying on regardless – parents, especially dads, are frequently impervious to the cringing embarrassment they are causing their offspring*): Did you say 'Jo'? Short for Josephine? A lovely name! We nearly called Laura Josephine. Either that or Arabella-Mary. But Laura was my mother's name. So we settled for Laura Winifred Pemberton. Very pretty, I'm sure you'll agree . . .

(Oh, Dad – PLEASE stop waffling! Isn't it time to watch the news, or something? No, apparently it is not . . .)

(Laura's dad takes off his jacket, to reveal that he is wearing that AWFUL yuk-brown M & S zip-up 'cardy' with the little suede shoulder patches . . .)

MR PEMBERTON: Has Laura told you about my farmyard

impressions? (*No. NO.*) You used to double up with laughter when I pretended to be a pig, didn't you, love?

(*USED TO, DAD – USED TO. Things which were side-splittingly hilarious when you were three, and mildly amusing when you were eight, have become hideously embarrassing now you are fifteen.*)

Distant but LOUD voice of little brother: MUM! MUM! THERE'S NO LOO PAPER!

Mr Pemberton (*unfazed*): MOOOOOO!!! That's a cow, by the way, not a pig.

(*Little Brother appears in the doorway with his trousers and underpants round his ankles. Laura wants to die.*)

3 DIFFERENT EMBARRASSING TYPES AND HOW TO DEAL WITH THEM

✦ The Jolly Dad (as encountered above). The word 'jolly' is associated with 'hockeysticks' and other words like 'super'. The state of jolliness is an uncool state to be in, but some dads don't seem to care. (You would not wish to be seen to be 'jolly' in public.) Father Christmas is jolly. He is not particularly cool, although he might be if he shaved off the stupid beard, had his nose pierced and looked mean and moody instead of going 'ho ho ho' all the time. You may be unlucky enough to have a dad who dresses up as Father Christmas for the kiddies (and all your friends KNOW who he is). Your dad may be normal most of the time, but he may BECOME jolly after a glass or two of his home-brewed beer. If you are really unlucky, he is permanently jolly (with or without beer), and wears a peaked cap with 'Kiss Me Quick' on it IN PUBLIC (pretend you are not with him). This type of dad thinks it is a good idea to demonstrate to your friends his skill at playing the spoons. You feel like hitting him over the head with a soup ladle.

UNCOOL FATHER CHRISTMAS

COOL FATHER CHRISTMAS

NOTE: You can also get a JOLLY mum. This type of mum is usually large, and wobbles when she laughs (like a jolly jelly). When she makes pancakes, she deliberately lets one land on her head. (How we all laughed.)

✦ THE CONCERNED MUM. This type of mum allows her deep maternal concern for your health and welfare to override every other consideration. As soon as you come through the door with your friends, she will home in on the cold sore beside your mouth. 'Here – keep still – let me put some cream on it. You MUST keep it dry – dear me, it's taking a long time to heal, isn't it? Perhaps I should ask the chemist if he's got anything else we could try . . . hold still a moment, let me have a closer look . . .' She relentlessly pursues the subject until you feel that your cold sore/spot is as big as a football, and all your friends are staring hard at it. It is a shame that her concern does not extend to protecting and preserving your Cool. There is no such thing as a Cool Sore, but, if there was, this type of mum would have some ointment for it. Unfortunately, an injury to your Cool does not show – but it is certainly painful.

FACT: If you try to act cool in front of your friends when there is a parent around, you can almost guarantee that they will suddenly shout out 'HAVE YOU DONE YOUR VERRUCA YET?' (or something similar).

✦ THE OBVIOUS PARENT (also known as the Glaringly

Obvious Parent). This type of parent wants the world (especially your friends, everyone at your school, and particularly Anyone-U-Fancy) to know that they are YOUR parent. In order to achieve this, they will go to great lengths, such as going shopping at one big store and buying the whole family the same matching sweaters and trousers. They may even buy the whole family identical jogging/cycling gear and insist that you all go out jogging/cycling together. They usually insist on going somewhere you KNOW your friends are likely to see you. Showing a complete lack of sensitivity, they will shout at you, 'There's Doug! He's a friend of yours, isn't he? Give him a wave!' This type of parent is frequently found at school events, where they like to say, in a loud voice, 'You're still my baby! Come and give your old mum a big kiss!'

✦ THE TACTLESS PARENT. Nearly every parent falls into this category, sooner or later. They are inclined to say things like, 'Goodness me, you look more and more like your grandpa every day!' This remark is especially unkind when it is addressed to a daughter, who has just spent the last two hours in her room with her friends, making herself look Supercool. They will also call your present boyfriend/girlfriend by the name of your previous boyfriend/girlfriend. Undeterred, they then go on to make matters worse by saying things like, 'Oh no, that was the last one, wasn't it?' and, 'I can't keep track of all these boyfriends/girlfriends! They keep changing!'

✦ The Hearty Parent. Closely related to the Jolly Parent, but possibly fitter (jolly fit). They like you to get up early so that the whole family can go for a brisk early-morning walk or jog together. When you get back, you are expected to eat a hearty breakfast. They also expect you to be enthusiastic about everything, just like they are:

Hearty mum: Oh, Aunty Maddy and Uncle Siggy are coming to stay for three weeks, with their six children! I'm not sure how we'll fit them all in, but we'll find a way. The three older girls can share *your* room, Lizzie! What fun! Isn't it exciting?

Lizzie: Er . . .

Hearty mum: Oh, come on! Show a little enthusiasm! (*She means LOTS of enthusiasm.*)

Lizzie: How wonderful.

Hearty mum: For goodness' sake – can't you manage just one little ecstatic grin and just one small whoop of excitement? Is it too much to ask?

The Hearty Parent has not yet worked out (and probably never will) that large (over-large) amounts of enthusiasm are incompatible with maintaining one's Cool. They still expect you to act like an excitable child (just as they do). They find your transition from enthusiastic youngster, with whom they identified, into a leading exponent of New Cool, which is totally baffling to them, a difficult one. Never mind – they will soon be off to their aerobics class, and you will be left in peace for a short while (and you can breathe a hearty sigh of relief).

✦ THE TRENDY PARENT.

TRENDY HAPPENIN' MUM *(or possibly Not Happenin')*: I'm really getting into The Groove! (*She grooves along to the beat, while stirring the cheese sauce.)*

OFFSPRING: It's not The Groove, Mum. It's just Groove. I think the cheese sauce is burning.

TRENDY DAD (LOW CQ)

Trendy, Not Happenin' dad: Hi, guys! I've just found my old flares. It's great to be wearing them again! I hear they're back in fashion! Whoops! The zip's just gone – they're a bit tight round the waist . . . (*What waist, Dad?*) Now – you can say what you like about the Bay City Rollers (*Who?*) but they certainly knew how to belt out a rollicking good song! I hear tartan's coming back into fashion . . . (*Coming* back *into fashion? It never was in fashion, apart from in Scotland amongst the warring clans who regularly slaughtered each other and went off with each other's kilts/women, etc.*)

4 HELPING YOUR PARENTS RESPECT YOUR SENSE OF STYLE AND YOUR MUSIC

Parents should respect your sense of style. When you were little, you didn't mind wearing the Noddy pyjamas which they provided, not to mention the frilly pink shorts with matching My Little Pony T-shirt (and this for a boy!). It was fun in those far-off days, when you dressed up in your parents' clothes. They should not expect you to want to do so any longer, least of all for FUN. You want to choose your own clothes, and you want to look cool. They have always been good at providing warm clothes, but not cool ones. They should try not to make any of the following remarks:

'I've got a lovely royal blue cardigan with gold buttons,

which would go beautifully with those trousers. Would you like to borrow it?'

'I'd love to see you looking really smart.'

'Goodness me – you look just like your mother did when she was your age!' (Surely not?!)

'That shirt would look quite smart if you did up all the buttons.'

Parents should also avoid tidying their offspring in public (tucking in labels, combing your hair and giving you a parting, taking a handkerchief or tissue and dabbing at some speck on your face with it, and so on). Being ultra tidy and smart is uncool. They may have got away with it when you were eight, and they scrubbed and polished your face, knees and shoes until they shone, neatly parted your hair or tied it up in ribbons, trussed you up in a little suit or frilly dress and dragged you off unwillingly to have tea with Great Aunt Millicent. But they can no longer get away with such behaviour. (There should be a law against it.) You have now grown more discerning, and you KNOW what you want to wear. Encourage them to try to accept this.

5 HELPING YOUR PARENTS GIVE YOU YOUR INDEPENDENCE

Parents should accept that they must not stand in the way of the onward march of New Cool. They have done a very thorough job over the last ten/fifteen years, bringing you up to be smart, enthusiastic, polite, keen and eager, with neatly-parted hair and a wardrobe full of clothes chosen by themselves. Now it is time for you to extricate yourself from all of this, and attempt to construct a New Cool Self. This will involve a period of re-adjustment for all involved, and your parent should help you by keeping . . . cool.

WARNING TO PARENTS : YOU SHOULD NOT EXPECT YOUR OFFSPRING TO BE EXACTLY LIKE YOU...

Your parents may further hamper your efforts to be cool by giving you brothers or sisters. Well, they didn't exactly *give* them to you, but they might just as well have done, judging by the way the brothers or sisters (especially the little ones) hang around you all the time, and refuse to go away when you want them to GO AWAY, because you would like some time alone with Person-U-Like. Older brothers and sisters are very similar

IT'S COOL WHEN OLDER SIBLINGS BRING HOME BEAUTIFUL FRIENDS

to the younger ones, only bigger. They are just as ugly/obnoxious/uncool, etc. (It is hard to believe that they are in any way related to YOU.) The redeeming feature of the older brother or sister is that they sometimes bring home their friends, some of whom are dazzlingly beautiful and very COOL indeed.

6 YOU, AN UNCOOL YULE AND THE FAMILY

'Keep your cool when all around are losing theirs.' Goodness knows what this means, but it sounds like a good idea, especially if you have parents who get easily stressed. This rule would apply particularly at Christmas, which is a bad time of year for all followers of New Cool.

You are herded together in one room with your entire family and hundreds of friends and relations whom you've never set eyes on before, and you are expected to be JOLLY. It is a recipe for arguments, stress and general mayhem. Ask for a Walkman (assuming you don't already have one) or the latest, most advanced headphones, so that you can plug yourself into the hi-fi system and block out the bickering, etc.

A new computer game might provide a distraction. Or even a steamy novel to lose yourself in as soon as you reach the sanctuary of your room. But whatever you ask for, don't be surprised if you get:

A socks;

B a new school bag;

C a leather-bound edition of the works of William Shakespeare, or

D a hand-knitted pullover in an uncool shade of sky blue.

Christmas is uncool – yes, OK, it CAN be fun, especially if you still get a stocking and your parent stuffs it with cool things like make-up, chocolate, your favourite rolled-up magazine, which takes up plenty of room in the stocking – parents make a note of this. You can hang up the most enormous bunch of mistletoe that ever was, and try to manoeuvre Person-U-Like to stand under it with you, and hope that they take the hint.

FESTIVE WARNING TO FESTIVE DAD: Resist the urge to kiss your daughter under the mistletoe in front of her friends.

UNCOOL YULE

Over-indulgence is another uncool aspect of Christmas. Everyone flops around looking and feeling totally stuffed (like the turkey). You hate turkey so you feed yours under the table to the dog/cat, who is later sick on the carpet, just as your mum wheels in the most enormous Christmas pudding . . .

All of the above can, of course, be applied to almost any family gathering or celebration (it doesn't *have* to be Christmas for your family to behave UNCOOLLY – they manage it fairly well all year round). Your best course of action is to retire to your room, or go for a walk with your friends (fresh air really *does* help).

New Year's Eve, on the other hand, can be cool, especially if you go paddling in the icy waters of the fountains in Trafalgar Square. You get to kiss people at midnight (this is cool if it is Person-U-Like, and mega UNCOOL if it is Uncle Harold or Aunty Sybil, who have both had far too much to drink). Make sure you are with someone you like as the clock (or Big Ben) strikes twelve . . .

7 HORRIBLE THINGS PARENTS DO AND YOUR RESPONSE

✦ Parents should NOT sing. This is especially embarrassing if they sing along to the radio, 'I love YOOOOO sweet banana . . .' (Actually, it is, 'I love you sweet na na na na . . .')

They should NOT play an imaginary guitar, pretend a wooden spoon is their microphone, or fall over the cat/ironing board as they strut and gyrate past you and your friends.

✦ Parents should NOT perform their yoga exercises in the middle of the living-room, wearing a stupid pink leotard which shows off their unsightly middle-aged spread (especially worrying behaviour if it is your dad). This is also embarrassing if they get stuck in one of the

yoga positions because their 'back has gone'.

✦ Parents should avoid taking off any of their clothes in public. They may be 'cuddly' (things are beginning to sag), but you would prefer it if your friends were not obliged to witness this depressing sight.

✦ They should not say, 'Look, everyone! I can waggle my ears!' If they insist on doing sad things like this, you can try saying, 'Sorry, guys, they're just sad/mad – fortunately it's not hereditary!' (As far as you know.)

✦ They should NOT shout at you to go and tidy your room, adding, 'I found a pair of socks under the bed that hadn't been washed for weeks!' There is no need for them to go into details, especially personal ones, if you have company. If they have something to say, they should talk to you quietly, out of earshot of your friends.

✦ Finally, parents should NOT bring out the family photo album, containing embarrassing photos of you as a baby with no clothes on; video of you using a potty for the first time; recording of your first burp or fart, etc, unless they have been specifically requested to do so (which is unlikely).

What You Can Do To Limit the Inevitable Embarrassment

✦ Turn up your own music sufficiently loudly so that you can't hear them if they start singing.

✦ If they are performing their yoga exercises or are in a state of undress, find a distraction (anything!). For example, 'Hey, guys! Look out of the window – that gorgeous babe in Year Twelve walks past our house every day about this time! Keep looking, or you might miss him/her!' While they are all staring out of the window, you have time to persuade your parent to go somewhere else/stop singing, etc.

Things to remember before you lose your cool completely:

✦ Everyone has families, or people they live with.

✦ Everyone must have had parents in the beginning, and most people are stuck with them for the next sixteen years.

✦ You may love them very much. And they love you. But they can still drive you mad.

✦ Most parents are uncool. But the fact that *they* are uncool should not affect YOU. Consider the Supercool Dude/Babe in Year Twelve (you spend most of your life considering them). Even they, presumably, have parents lurking somewhere in the background. But it hasn't cramped *their* style. Why should it cramp yours?

8 YOU GREW UP TOO FAST

Avoid confrontation. Be polite and charming to the old and wrinkly. Remember that they are probably having difficulties accepting that you are changing and no longer want to bounce in from school every day straight into their loving arms (parents are creatures of habit, and they often feel comfortable with what they are used to).

YOU AT EIGHT

CHILD RETURNS FROM SCHOOL, SMILING BRIGHTLY: Hi, Mum!

MUM: Hello, love! Had a good day?

CHILD: Not bad, thanks. Mrs Pertwee says I'm doing really well at maths – and I scored a goal in football/hockey. It was brill! I got six credits today.

MUM: Oh, well done! Let me give you a big hug!

(They enjoy a BIG HUG.)

(Nine Years Later. {For you it is nine years. For them it is nothing – only days.} Same child returns from school. It is not smiling. It says nothing.)

MUM: Hello, love! Had a good day?

(No reply.)

MUM: Everything all right, love?

CHILD: Yeah. Guess so.

MUM: Get any credits today?

CHILD *(Which is no longer a child, but is now a fully-fledged Supercool Dude/Babe)*: Ten, I think. What about it?

MUM: Oh, you ARE clever! Let me give you a big hug!

SUPERCOOL DUDE/BABE: Yeah, OK – but mind my hair. I'm going up to my room to chill out for a while. I've got my mobile with me, in case anyone wants me.

REMEMBER: A parent who is not yet used to the New Cool You, may mistake coolness for rudeness. This can lead to angry scenes. So make sure you answer them when they talk to you, smile occasionally (cultivate a Cool Smile), and ask them if they've had a good day, or some other friendly inquiry, to put them at their ease. Handling your parents coolly is a skill which you can practise. If you can handle your parents and STILL keep your cool, then you really ARE a cool dude! In other words, if you can cope with parents, then you can probably cope with most things. Your home may be one of the BEST places to practise being cool. It is the first challenge to your cool that you are likely to encounter. You can do it! You can have parents and STILL be COOL!

CHAPTER 3

Cool Confidence – How To Build It

You may or may not have successfully risen to the First Challenge to your Cool, which came in the shape of parents and family. They may well prove to be the only people in your life who can still make you feel uncool when you are eighteen, twenty-one, twenty-four, thirty-two, forty-nine, etc. Don't worry about it. Feeling uncool with your family should just remind you of how exceedingly cool you are the rest of the time. (You can always go home to practise your Basic Skills of Cool . . .)

The Second Challenge to your Cool is posed by the wider world outside the home (friends, school, work, people in general). Home may then be seen as a sanctuary, where you can take refuge when you need to regain your cool. At home you can relax and be totally uncool for a while, if you wish. You can wear your much-loved fluffy tartan slippers, which make your feet look about a hundred years old, but they are really comfortable – and comforting. You just wouldn't be seen DEAD in them by anyone you know. Parents don't matter (this is not meant in an unpleasant way. Some parents fall into the same category as comfortable old slippers – but don't tell this to the Trendy Dad).

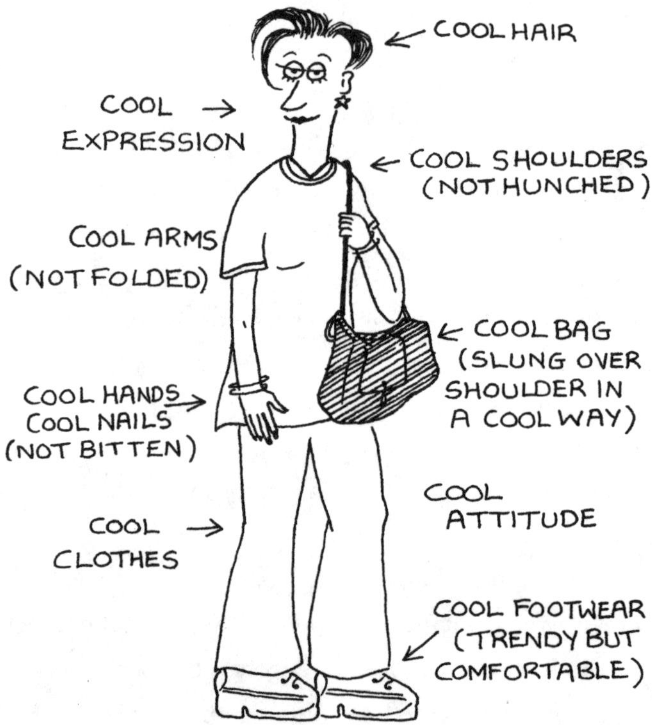

COOL BABE

But what do you do when it is time to stuff the fluffy slippers firmly under the bed, and exchange them for the cool trainers in which you are about to step out into the world? You need to be PREPARED. So how do you prepare?

The Essence of Cool is CONFIDENCE. Loads of it. Bucketsful. But if you only have a tiny thimbleful of it, don't worry. That is a good start. Now is the time to start Confidence-Building Exercises.

In front of the mirror, with no one around to put you off, is a good place to begin. Here you can practise your Basic Skills of Cool.

BASIC SKILLS OF COOL

1 RELAX Notice if your shoulders are hunched up somewhere round your ears. Not very relaxed, are you? Let them drop. Do some shoulder circling, bend your neck gently from side to side (but not too far in case something goes click and you get stuck). Flex your fingers several times. Splay your toes. Breeeeeathe . . . Good. That's the relaxation exercises sorted. You should do them at least six times every day – at school, at home, walking the dog, talking on the phone, sitting on the loo . . .

2 COOL SMILE Practise your Cool Smile. What exactly IS a Cool Smile? This is a difficult one. In order to achieve a Cool Smile, you could try the following: give yourself a most enormous, manic, Children's TV-presenter-style cheesy grin in the mirror (this is an Uncool Smile). Now let your face relax. The muscles around your mouth have all been stretched, and they should slowly subside and settle into something that might just be a Cool Smile (not forced, not trying too hard – but relaxed).

HAIR SENSE

A BAD HAIR DAY CAN MAKE YOU FEEL UNCOOL

BIG HAIR

3 APPEARANCE Make the most of your appearance. Don't worry if you have a few spots. There are some people whose faces resemble the surface of a volcanic planet (full of craters, erupting bits), but they still manage to be Real Cool Dudes. But a bad hair day can make you feel lousy and uncool, so do something about the hair. Wash it, condition it (LOADS of conditioner so that it is as soft and shiny and silky as . . . as a silky thing). Have it cut into a cool style. If you are a boy, you would be well advised to avoid the local hairdressing salon where they will wrap you up in a floral gown and make you look completely stupid and uncool while all the old ladies in curlers cluck over you and your mates laugh and point through the window. You should also avoid the local barber's, where they will make you look like your dad. Your best option is to go to a trendy, youthful hairdressing establishment where you know the stylists have your best interests at heart, and will do their best to give you Cool Hair. If you can't afford a trip to the hairdresser, or you are having trouble with your hair and it refuses to look cool no matter what you do, your best option is probably to:

A Have it all cut off (but be careful about this – cropped hair or a shaven head suits some people, but not all. And your parents may react in a very uncool way . . .).

B Wear a Cool Hat. If you can't afford a Cool Hat, why not dredge up a long-forgotten bobble hat from the bottom of a drawer (you loved it when you were six), and cut off the bobble. Hey presto! Instant Cool Hat!

UNCOOL HAT

WARNING: Do not try this with your little brother/sister's bobble hat – they will burst into tears, and your parents will react uncoolly again . . .

C You can force your hair to behave coolly by using loads of gel, etc.

4 COOL GLASSES It is no longer true that boys don't make passes at girls who wear glasses (or vice versa). You can get some really cool frames which will simply add to your Cool Image (possibly at an uncool price – talk to your parents in a nice voice, and offer to do the washing-up for the next six weeks . . .). Contact lenses can be cool, except when they get dropped on the floor, and you end up on your hands and knees searching for them.

5 DO IT EVER SO SLOWLY You may have observed that Cool Dudes/Babes move in slow motion. Even when the rest of the world is rushing around in frantic, ever-decreasing circles, tearing their hair out (what a waste, after spending all that money on a Cool Cut), the Cool Dude or Babe is never in a hurry. They wander past, moving easily, languidly, even sexily.

NOTE: A sexy walk does NOT involve wiggling your bottom consciously from side to side like a hyperactive

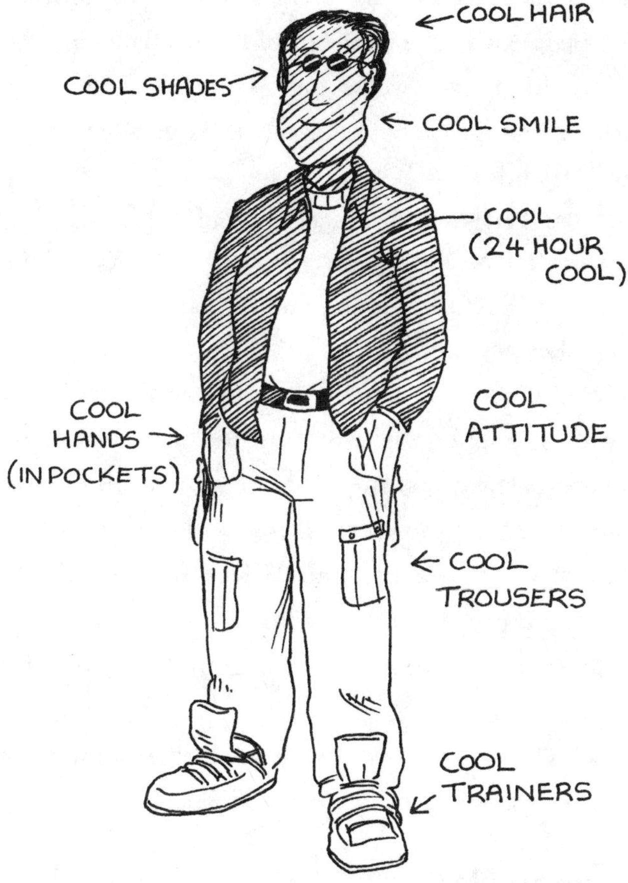

COOL DUDE

duck. If you are cool, you will be sexy, you will move sexily, you don't need to think about it.

Practise your slow, relaxed Cool Walk around the room. Try not to fall over the cat. You can learn a lot about how to move coolly, and behave coolly, by observing other people. Check out the Cool Dudes/Babes at school (mostly in Years Twelve and Thirteen) and observe (without being too obvious about it) your older brother/sister's friends.

6 COOL THINKING Practise Cool Thinking. Tell yourself, 'I KNOW I look good . . . I KNOW I look good . . . I KNOW I look good . . .' and enjoy the way this makes you feel.

Avoid Uncool Thinking: 'Oh my god, I look like a purple hippopotamus! My bum looks ENORMOUS! Everyone's staring at me! They're all laughing! I can't stand it!' This kind of thinking will turn you into a nervous wreck, and it is all WRONG. You DON'T look like a purple hippopotamus, and no one is staring at you. You need to train your brain to Think Cool.

Cool Thinking: Wow! People are looking at me. They must like the way I did my hair. I *like* being looked at . . .

You can practise Cool Thinking with your friends . . .

YOU: I'm feeling good today!

FRIEND: You're looking pretty good!

YOU: You're not looking too bad yourself!

FRIEND: We're pretty cool, huh?

YOU: Yesss!

ANOTHER FRIEND: Oh, for god's sake – SHUT UP!

PLEASE NOTE: You should not expect your friends to be COOL the whole time. You should also be able to relax with them and have a good laugh at how uncool life/parents/school/things in general can be at times. Laughter is COOL (as long as it is not hysterical or forced, or at someone else's expense). Confident is good, but you should avoid arrogance. Arrogant is not cool, it's just irritating.

LOUD, FORCED LAUGHTER MAY NOT BE YOUR BEST OPTION (TRYING TOO HARD IS UNCOOL . . .)

COOL HOBBIES

- ✦ Play an instrument well.
- ✦ Learn to yo-yo or juggle really well.
- ✦ Dance.
- ✦ Go skateboarding/rollerblading (boarding or blading)

or cycling (but make sure your bike is big enough for you – you will not look cool on your little sister's cycle, pedalling along with your knees out at right angles . . .).

NOTE: Of course, if you fancy a hobby that isn't usually recognised as cool, you can do it and just revel in being different and individual. If you're confident and approach it in a cool way, most things can be made to seem cool . . . (so go and get that tuba!).

If you run out of Cool Things To Do, remember that you can always take the dog/cat/hamster for a walk . . .

JUGGLING IS COOL, IF YOU CAN DO IT PROPERLY...

FRIENDS AND COOL

The next Confidence-Building Exercise is to involve friends. Invite them home to meet the New Cool You. They have probably already admired your hair (this boosts your confidence). Have a sort through your clothes drawers with them, or go shopping together, so that you can try out some new looks (you don't need to spend a fortune – perhaps a New Cool Hat is all you need). Ask their opinions, but be guided mainly by what YOU feel good in. If they tease you, practise maintaining your cool. If you KNOW you look good (and you do), you don't need to rely on the opinions of others (which has always been confusing, since everyone's opinions are different). Treat your friends to your Cool *Knowing* Smile.

OVERCOMING SHYNESS AND BEING LAID-BACK

Of course, being totally laid-back is easier said than done. When you are first plunged into a school (or other social situation) full of people who all *seem* to have more confidence than you have, it can be a deeply intimidating experience. But remember that this is an illusion. All of these people are HUMAN (apart from the strange boy in Year Eight who may well be from the Planet Yark), and they are all subject to the same doubts and insecurities as yourself. If you suffer from crippling shyness (and you fear you will *never* be cool), try thinking about how other people are feeling, instead of concentrating on your own lack of confidence. Become an observer of others (this does not mean standing right beside them, staring hard), and notice how they cover up their basic shyness (which undoubtedly exists). Some of them are over-loud (this is not so cool), while others are more laid-back. Their whole physical attitude is relaxed, and they don't seem too bothered about anything (this may be a form of self-protection, as they avoid getting too involved in anything, and keep themselves distanced – this *is* cool, but they may miss out on some of the fun, as well as avoiding stress). Others just have a quiet, non-pushy, friendly attitude, which is probably coolest of all. Being truly cool, as opposed to acting it, means you don't fret if not everyone seems to like you instantly. This takes practice!

THE UNCOOL SCENE

SUNI: Hey! Do you like my new Play Station? Mum and Dad gave it to me for my birthday.

JEZ: It's OK. Actually, it's pretty naff. I bet it didn't cost THAT much. You should see my new Games Centre. It's got EVERYTHING. Mum and Dad had to have an extra room built on to the house to install it. It's fully networked so up to forty people can sit and play the same game together. It cost THE EARTH. And it wasn't even my birthday when they gave it to me.

SUNI: So? Do you think you're BIG or something?

JEZ: I'm bigger than you are.

SUNI: Aren't.

JEZ: Am.

SUNI: Aren't.

This is very UNCOOL indeed. If you wish to be a leading light in New Cool, you must avoid this sort of behaviour at all costs. (Boys are particularly prone to it – girls have more sense. I throw in this sexist comment just to wind you up . . .)

THE COOL SCENE

SUNI: Do you like my new Play Station?

JEZ: Yes, it's great! Can I have a go? Why don't you come round and see my new Games Centre one day? It's pretty amazing.

SUNI: Yeah. That'd be cool.

In this scene, both boys avoid bragging, showing off and falling out. They keep any feelings of envy or irritation to themselves. So – another Basic Ingredient of Cool is not allowing people to get to you, or wind you up. If you allow yourself to be wound up too easily by your friends and other people, you will be permanently losing your Cool (which is exhausting). It may even result in Total Loss of Cool (for which you may need to see the doctor).

COOL WAYS TO DEAL WITH THE SHOW-OFF

It is not necessary to try to *impress* friends, because, if they are real friends, they already like you for yourself (they are already impressed by your friendly, relaxed attitude). If you find you are faced with a show-off:

✦ When they are in full brag mode, yawn loudly and stretch luxuriously (this gets rid of tension brought on by being exposed to Uncool Behaviour), and quietly wander away . . .

✦ If, for instance, they are boasting about their new hi-tech yo-yo, complete with flashing lights, and what they can do with it, quietly produce your own yo-yo (which needn't be anything special – or it might be) and perform an absolutely spectacular trick (which you have been practising at home for days). Quietly put it away in your pocket again.

If you are going to play someone at their own game, you must be *certain* that you can go one better (otherwise it is better NOT to risk failing in front of everyone), and you must do so casually, almost absent-mindedly, as if your mind is actually on other things and you really don't have to try . . . This

PEOPLE CAN WIND YOU UP

kind of behaviour is risky, and falls into the category of Advanced Cool. You should make sure that you have mastered Basic Cool first (relax, don't try too hard, and don't let other people wind you up – like a yo-yo).

A RECIPE FOR COOL

All you need to do now is to follow the Recipe for Cool, which is as follows . . .

The Basic Ingredients of Cool:

an extra large dollop of concentrated CONFIDENCE;
a relaxed attitude;
a Cool Smile;
a Cool Hairstyle;
Cool clothes/make-up, etc;
a Cool bodyspray/deodorant;
a Cool Way of Walking;
a Cool Way of Talking;
Cool Things to Talk About and
another hefty dollop of CONFIDENCE.

METHOD

Combine all the above ingredients, and mix well (with friends/people at school, etc.). Turn into Hot Stuff. Chill out for a while. Leave to COOL for the rest of your life. You now have a Cool Attitude. Garnish with a healthy

sprinkling of humour and laughter, and your New Cool will serve you well. This is a very simple recipe to follow, but don't despair if you boil over occasionally, burn (remember to use suncream) or go slightly flat. This is only to be expected. Just mix up all the above ingredients again, with an extra helping of confidence (a pep talk from a friend? A morale-boosting visit to the shops?) and leave to rise above the hassle and stress of everyday life. Chill out on a bed or sofa for several hours, and you'll be fine. (Plenty of rest and a good, nutritious diet are also important ingredients of Cool, and should not be overlooked. You can't function properly without them. They may not sound cool but it's how you do them – instead of saying, 'Oh, I must have an early night. I like to be tucked up in bed by nine with a mug of hot milk,' try saying, 'Must hit the sack. I have to look good tomorrow.' You may observe that the Cool Dude does not allow events in his life to spoil his appetite, or disturb his Cool Sleep/Beauty Sleep.)

COOL ATTITUDE AND PRACTICE SITUATIONS

Now that you have a Cool Attitude, you need to try it out in a variety of different situations. You build up your confidence by pushing yourself into situations which you may initially feel nervous about. Once you realise that you can handle them, you feel stronger and more confident.

TEST YOUR COOL
SITUATION NO. 1

Laura Pemberton decides to go along to the youth club for the first time. She feels nervous, because she doesn't know what to expect. Will everyone else, apart from her, be cool and confident and know exactly what to do and say? Will everyone else, apart from her, have a boyfriend/girlfriend? Will everyone stare at her?

WHAT CAN LAURA DO TO PREPARE HERSELF FOR THIS NEW SITUATION?

✦ She should be realistic and avoid getting over-excited or wound up. It is most unlikely that she will be confronted by a room full of cool, confident, beautiful people, all with boyfriends or girlfriends, all knowing exactly what to do and say. It is much more likely that she will be confronted by a room full of people who are basically like herself (possibly not so cool). She should remember that most of them probably share the same doubts, insecurities and occasional lapses in confidence, and most of them will be doing their best to cover this up, and act COOL.

✦ If she feels nervous, she should ask a friend (or friends) to go along with her. They can have a laugh getting ready together, boosting each other's morale, and it will be a lot easier for them to act COOL if they have each other's company and support.

✦ She can practise and rehearse simple chat-up lines and conversation-openers. 'Hi!' is a good one (keep it simple). A second chat-up line to fall back on is a good idea, in case they both say 'Hi!' and conversation stops there. She should remark on something the other person is wearing/carrying/doing, such as, 'That's a really cool watch. Where did you get it?'

✦ She should prepare herself for a shortage of conversation by practising cool gestures and body language, such as running her hands through her hair to push it back from her face, straightening a belt or readjusting a scarf. (Not all body language is appropriate: you should resist having a good old scratch.)

THE COOL (?) SCENE

Laura, Skye and Pippi arrive at the youth club and find that there is no pressure. They wander in casually. A few boys look in their direction, while others seem more interested in playing pool. Some of the boys show off, but they are quite funny. One or two of them are quite fanciable. But there is certainly no question of wall-to-wall Supercool Dudes and Babes. Some of the girls are friendly, and some aren't. It is a bit like school, without the necessity to wear uniform and do work. Laura, Skye and Pippi feel relaxed and cool. They can handle it. They will come back next week, and practise their New Cool and see what effect it has on the boys (especially the Fanciable Ones).

TEST YOUR COOL
SITUATION NO. 2

Suni Lal has won a competition to visit a recording studio to meet the lead singer of Groove, a band he admires.

The lead singer's name is Lisa, and she is very glamorous and Ultra Cool. Suni is terrified that he will do or say something stupid, and make a complete idiot of himself.

WHAT CAN SUNI DO TO PREPARE HIMSELF FOR THIS SITUATION?

✦ He can rehearse in advance what he is going to say to Lisa, such as, 'I think your band's really cool.' If he keeps it simple, and doesn't try too hard to impress, there shouldn't be a problem.

✦ He can prepare himself by doing relaxation exercises, and by taking a few slow, deep breaths. He can imagine he is breathing OUT all his doubts and insecurities, and breathing IN confidence.

✦ He should try to remember that even the most glamorous and Supercool individual is still a human

TRY TO IMAGINE THE GLAMOROUS/SUPERCOOL ONE DOING SOMETHING UNCOOL ...

being, like himself. It might help Suni to imagine Lisa feeding her dog (if she has one) or doing her weekly shopping and buying boring things like kitchen roll and more dog food. (You can take this a step further by imagining the Glamorous/Supercool One sitting on the loo – this is an awful thing to do, of course, but remarkably effective.)

THE COOL SCENE

Suni is introduced to Lisa. She is very friendly and talks so much that he doesn't really need to say anything. He manages to say, 'I really like your new album – it's cool!' Lisa looks genuinely pleased and touches his arm. 'And I think *you're* really cool, Suni!' Suni tries to give a Cool Smile, but it breaks into a wide, ecstatic grin, and his eyes shine. His heart is beating like a sledgehammer, but he doesn't care any longer. He is a Cool Dude. He can handle it. No sweat, man! Suddenly he wishes he could meet loads of glamorous and Cool People. There is NOTHING to worry about.

COOL QUIZ

Friends give you Confidence, which is the Essence of Cool. But occasionally Friends can Wind You Up. Do you deal with this coolly or uncoolly? To find out, do the following simple quiz:

1 Two friends are talking together in hushed tones. They obviously don't want you to hear what they are saying, and you suspect that they are talking about YOU. How do you react?

A You hop about from foot to foot in a frenzy of agitation and curiosity, shouting, 'What are you talking about? Tell me! TELL ME! It's NOT fair! You're shutting me out, and I hate you!' You may even burst into tears, or storm off in a mood, banging the furniture, kicking a chair over and slamming a door.

B You pick up a book and pretend to read, but your ears are twitching violently in an effort to overhear what is being said.

C You quietly wander away. If they don't want to tell you something, you don't want to know. And if they are going to behave stupidly, you can do without them until they start treating you like a friend again.

2 A friend tells you something that you don't want to hear, such as the fact that Babe-U-Fancy has started going out with someone else. How do you react?

A You immediately burst into tears, or start hissing and spitting with rage, before shouting, 'IT'S NOT FAIR! I HATE EVERYONE AND EVERYTHING!!!' You then run out of the room, or sit and brood with a face like thunder or an expression of utter despair.

B You shout, 'So what?! I DON'T CARE. Do you think I CARE? Well, you're WRONG!!! So there!' You carry on like this for the next forty minutes, or longer.

C You say, 'Oh?' This is probably ALL you say. You may pick up a book and start reading, or say that you feel in need of some fresh air, and you might go for a walk.

3 Someone (possibly NOT a friend) makes an unkind personal remark, such as that your nose looks even bigger now that it has a spot on the end of it. How do you react?

A You burst into tears, or march out of the room, slamming the door behind you.

B You hurl an insult back, such as, 'Not as big as your mouth, frog-face!'

C You DON'T react.

4 You go shopping with friends and try on some trousers which you really like. But one of your friends says they don't suit you/make you look stupid. How do you react?

A You become very stressed, and tell your friend that they (the friend) are horrible, and that *they* look stupid in what *they* are wearing.

B You decide not to get the trousers, and worry for the rest of the shopping trip about WHY they didn't suit you.

C You say, 'Oh, I rather like them!' You say this in a friendly and pleasant way, and you don't worry about it. You look forward to wearing the trousers.

5 Your mates are daring you to do something stupid, like kicking an empty Coke can through the open staffroom window. What do you do?

A You take aim, and kick the Coke can straight into the staffroom.

B You exclaim, 'Oh, NO! I would NEVER do a thing like that! It would be a terribly stupid thing to do, likely to land me in a lot of trouble, and I might hurt someone. And besides, it is certainly against the rules. How could you possibly even suggest such a thing?'

C You say, 'I don't think so. I've got other things to do.' And you wander away, hands in pockets, whistling, kicking the Coke can along the ground.

6 Your friends are teasing you about Dude/Babe-U-Fancy: 'You really LIKE him/her, don't you? Look – you're blushing bright red! You've really got the hots, haven't you? Go on – admit it!' How do you react?

A You shout, 'Shut up! Leave me alone!' And you storm out of the room, slamming the door.

B You protest, 'No, I DON'T like him/her! And I am NOT blushing! I NEVER blush! So you're WRONG. OK?'

C You smile, and say, 'You guys can read me like a book, can't you?' Then you have a long, luxurious stretch and maybe say something like, 'So what do you reckon my chances are, then?'

MOSTLY A'S: There will not be many doors left on their hinges by the time you've finished. You must stop slamming doors, bursting into tears, and generally overreacting and losing your cool too easily and too frequently. You should pause to consider that friends and others are occasionally guilty of deliberately trying to provoke you, or wind you up. In fact, the more they realise that they CAN wind you up, the more tempted they may be to do so. There may also be one or two troublemakers around who will spread rumours and gossip that is not necessarily true. Don't give THEM the satisfaction of seeing you lose your cool. If you don't react (this may be difficult, so you need to practise – take a deep breath, count to forty-seven, and so on), the troublemakers will soon lose interest, and give up. Your friends may occasionally tease you, but another part of being Cool is learning to accept a certain amount of teasing without getting grumpy or stroppy.

WARNING: If your friends dare you to do something stupid, and you are tempted to do it just in order to impress them, take a few moments to ask yourself if it is worth it. You shouldn't NEED to impress your friends. (Question: Why aren't *they* prepared to do whatever it is? Answer: Because *they* don't want to get into trouble, but they are curious to see what will happen to you . . .) The chances are that you will get caught by a teacher/parent or other adult who will tell you off in front of everyone, which will make you look and feel decidedly UNCOOL. Remember that Cool Rules state that it is better to stick to the School Rules rather than risk being make to look STUPID. Cool Rules also state that you should not try too hard to impress. If you feel that you are being pushed into doing something that you are not sure about, it is better to say that you have other things to do, and just walk away (remember your Cool Way of Walking – relaxed, unhurried . . .).

MOSTLY B'S: The more you try to deny something that is evidently the case, or pretend that you don't care, the more obvious it becomes that you *do* care. You are a soft target for anyone who wants to have some fun at your expense. Don't let them do it. It is better, and more cool, not to react to the deliberate wind-up (disappointing for others, of course, but they will have to find some other means of amusing themselves). It is uncool to hurl insults, unless they are particularly pithy or funny – but if you are not quite in the same league as Oscar Wilde, leave it out. Cool Rules also stipulate that it is mega UNCOOL to be a goody-goody (a goody two-shoes, or a goody two-trainers . . .).

MOSTLY C'S: Yo! You are a Cool Dude indeed (or a Cool Babe, or simply a Cool Customer). You have worked out that it is better not to give too much away, because there are always unscrupulous people around who will seize on your weaknesses and prey on your vulnerability. You need to choose your friends carefully before you confide too much in them (well, you already know that). You have also worked out that if there are one or two things that are patently obvious (such as the fact that you fancy someone like mad), there is not much point in hotly denying it. It is better to smile, say as little as possible, and show the world that you can handle it. You are also aware that even the Coolest Dude feels insecure occasionally, and that you have no need to prove anything to other people, who are likely to be just as vulnerable as yourself.

If you *do* lose your cool occasionally (and most people do), it is useful to have somewhere to go where you can quietly regain your composure (an old-fashioned word for Cool). This is usually possible at home, where you can retreat to your room, or go out for a walk. It is more challenging to find somewhere quiet at school, where you can be alone for a while. Try the library, or a music practice room (this is easier if you actually have an instrument to play). You can always lock yourself in the loo, but this may not be the ideal place to feel COOL in. (School loos are traditionally uncool places, with an uncool smell . . .)

As you face each new challenge to your Cool and overcome it, so your confidence will grow. There will occasionally be times when this goes wrong. You may feel overwhelmed, or you may be trying so hard that you don't really enjoy yourself, or you may feel that you've failed miserably. Remember that this happens to everyone from time to time, and you just have to keep going. It will get much better, soon. Especially when you learn to deal with the next major challenge to your cool – that posed by SCHOOL.

CHAPTER 4

How To Be Cool At School

The world 'school' rhymes with 'cool'. But there the similarity ends. School and Cool are worlds apart, and the challenge is to somehow bring them together, as far as is humanly possible . . .

School is a word which you usually mention in the same breath as a groan or a heavy sigh. Not many people wake up on Monday morning and shout, 'Wow! School! Oh, goody, goody, goody! Lucky, lucky me!' This is definitely an uncool way to start the week (in fact, it is totally mad).

MAKING YOUR SCHOOL SOUND COOL

It is necessary to be cool *about* school. A Cool Attitude to school is essential. You may feel that the very fact

that you go to school at all is deeply damaging to your Cool. This needn't be the case. There is not much point in pretending that you don't go to school, because most people do. It is also the place where you may form your closest friendships, and Friends Are Cool (most of the time).

Consider the following conversation:

COOL DUDE/BABE (*chatting you up – YESSS!*): So, what do you do with your time?

YOU: Oh, I go to school. And then I come home again.

(Hmm. This is accurate, but uninteresting. You are making yourself sound – and feel – uncool.)

COOL DUDE/BABE (*trying again – he or she must really like you*): No, go on, tell me – what do you really do with your time?

You: Oh, there's a crowd I hang out with at school. They're cool, and we have loads of fun, especially during metalwork.

(*This is better, although you could obviously improve on it.*)

School itself may not be cool (school uniform is the very Essence of Uncool), but there are various aspects of school which ARE cool.

WHAT IS COOL AND UNCOOL ABOUT SCHOOL?

COOL

✦ The gorgeous Babes and Cool Dudes in Year Twelve.

✦ Some teachers (OK, maybe not at *your* school . . .).

✦ Seeing your friends every day.

✦ If your school is an enlightened place, it may organise fun activities, such as end-of-term discos/parties, or even sponsored kisses (on the cheek only, please).

✦ The canteen. This may not *seem* like the coolest of places, especially if someone starts a food fight and you end up wearing a half-eaten jam sandwich as a hat. But the food has improved since the days when the only item on the menu in most schools was cabbage which had been boiling for the last six days. If the food has improved, the same cannot necessarily be said of the company. But who knows? Perhaps you can carefully manoeuvre your way across the canteen and find a place

UPDATED VERSION OF
OLIVER TWIST

to sit at the same table as Babe/Dude-U-Like. You can then eat your turkey burger in a sexy way, and hope that they notice you.

UNCOOL

✦ The SMELL. This is a rich and strange and frankly disgusting combination of various aromas: rotten old boiled cabbage (ghostly cabbage, wafting down through the centuries . . .), stinking socks and unwashed PE kit, the odd boy or girl who does not believe in washing, the History teacher's REVOLTING perfume (you can smell it EVERYWHERE) and a hint of dead mouse (it escaped from the Biology lab and was never located).

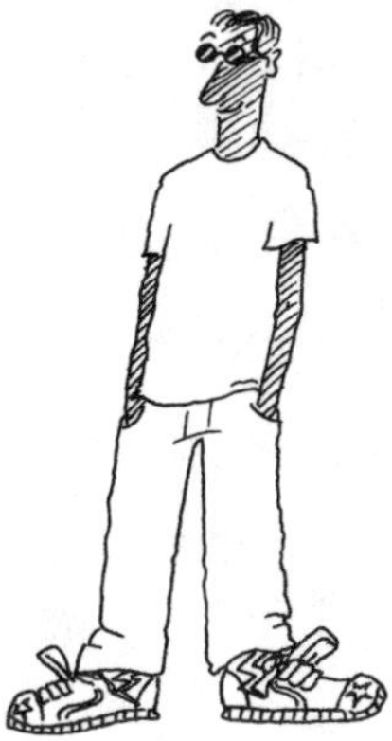

COOL TRAINERS

UNCOOL TRAINERS (RECENTLY REMOVED FROM FEET)

UNCOOL SOCKS (ASSORTED. ODD. SOMETIMES MISTAKEN FOR SOMETHING DEAD)

SOLVING UNCOOL SCHOOL PROBLEMS

SOLUTION TO THE SMELL PROBLEM

Use your favourite deodorant or bodyspray so that you smell really COOL. If someone says, 'Wow! What's that fantastic smell?' as you walk into the room, it will boost your confidence enormously. (In the more unlikely event that everyone leaves the room when you walk in, you will know that you have chosen the WRONG deodorant/bodyspray.) Go shopping with a few friends and try out some different scents so that you can pinpoint the most popular one that *everyone* seems to like (this is usually the most expensive . . . Talk to your parents in a

COOL
RULES
(O.K?)

TAKE YOUR HANDS OUT OF YOUR POCKETS !!
SCHOOL
RULES
(O.K.?)
LAST YEAR'S SCHOOL TROUSERS

COOL – OR WHAT?

very nice voice, and offer to do the washing-up – and tidy your room – for the next ten weeks).

When you go to school, you have to observe the rules. I am not just talking about School Rules. I am also talking about Cool Rules (also known as Cool Rools – cool spelling). These do not necessarily coincide. It is a question of bending (not breaking) both slightly so that they meet in the middle. One of the main areas where you can do this is with school uniform.

THE UNIFORM

If your uniform is mainly black, you are lucky. Black is cool. It is more of a challenge to be Cool in ghastly green or murky mulberry (although I've heard that murky mulberry is going to be *the* colour for next autumn . . .). Your main aim is to avoid looking like the idiot in the photo on the cover of the School Prospectus, who looks as though he has been washed, ironed, starched and pressed into his school uniform, which he obviously wears with PRIDE. His shoes gleam. He is uncool.

HE WEARS HIS UNIFORM WITH PRIDE

Cool Rules (as opposed to School Rules) state that your uniform should look 'lived-in', which indicates that you still *have* a life, and are not merely a stuffed school uniform, standing or sitting to attention. The 'lived-in and still alive' look is achieved by not looking *too* smart. Perhaps your shirt is not tucked in (unless you are Jeremy Witherspoon, in which case it is firmly tucked into your underpants). One or two buttons (at the cuffs or the collar) might be left undone. If you are a girl, a very long skirt is cool, and so is a very short skirt (especially on a freezing day in winter), but you may feel uncool in a skirt which is just below knee-length (there is something very *sensible* about this length, which hints at prunes for breakfast, a conscientious attitude to homework, and going to bed early with a mug of malted bedtime drink). Most schools also allow girls to wear trousers, especially in the winter, as long as they are in the same colour as the rest of the uniform (ghastly green trousers – mmm. . . !).

Then there is the School Bag. Fortunately, this does NOT have to be the same colour as the rest of the uniform (imagine a ghastly green bag). Your choice of school bag is governed more by Cool Rules than by School Rules. There is usually a particular style of bag which is considered trendy, so you might get one of those. Yes – equip yourself with a Cool Bag (NOT a plastic carrier for frozen foods . . .).

Wearing your uniform with COOL (as opposed to with PRIDE) is a step in the right direction, but it is difficult to keep your cool in a place where there are bells going off in all directions, and crowds of people pushing, shoving and shouting in the corridors, and stressed teachers, and some individuals, scurrying to and fro with anxious expressions on their faces, muttering, 'I'm lost!' or 'I'm late! I'm late!' like the White Rabbit out of *Alice In Wonderland.*

If you wish to be truly cool, you must think of yourself as being at the still centre of all this frantic activity. Remember your Cool Way of Walking, which means that there is no need to hurry. You walk at a slow, relaxed pace, chatting with your friends, ignoring the hustle and the bustle around you. (The leaders of New Cool are seldom, if ever, *early* for lessons . . . But at least they don't run the risk of tripping over and falling flat on their faces in their haste to get to Biology.) You might say 'Hi!' to someone you know as you pass them (they are hurrying in the opposite direction). If you want your friends to think you are immensely popular, try saying 'Hi!' or 'Yo!' to all sorts of people as you pass them (regardless of whether you know them or not).

COOL AT SPORT

Don't worry. Being *cool* at sport is NOT necessarily the same as being good at sport – although that often helps. It means having a relaxed attitude towards playing sport, which probably means that you will enjoy it more (although racing up and down a muddy field in hot pursuit of a ball is not everyone's cup of tea, and some of you Cool Dudes out there may already have decided that it is NOT for you).

UNCOOL ATTITUDES TO SPORT

✦ Wanting to win at all costs for the glory of the school (a laudable attitude – but not cool).

✦ Wanting to win at all costs for any reason. If you are too fiercely competitive, you end up screaming and

SERIOUSLY UNCOOL ATTITUDE TO SPORT

shouting like a maniac at other people to catch/pass the ball, and you get totally stressed if they miss it/you miss it/you lose. You end up with wild, staring eyes, mad hair, and sweat pouring off you. You lose your temper with the referee/the umpire, and hurl your tennis racket/ hockey stick down with such force that it breaks. You lie on the ground, kicking and screaming. This is if you lose (at anything from tennis to tiddlywinks). If you win, you leap around like a hyperactive baboon, hugging and kissing everyone and everything in sight, including the muddy, churned up ground.

WHAT IS COOL ABOUT SPORT

✦ If you have natural talent, you may turn into a School Sporting Hero or Heroine. This is quite a cool thing to be, and you might even have your own fan club of people who admire you. If you have natural talent, you can be relaxed and cool about your sport, without getting stressed by it. You enjoy it, you excel at it, you are COOL at it. Lucky you.

✦ You can also enjoy sport without having to be brilliant at it: 'It is not the winning or the losing, but the taking part that matters.' This is a reasonably cool attitude. But if you are too laid-back (taking time out during a match to lie down in the middle of the field/ court for a few minutes' snooze), you may incur the wrath of the heartier types who believe in getting up at six a.m. to start training for the match, and keeping on their toes the whole time.

✦ Sports which you can do on your own can be cool, such as swimming. If you are a girl, you can glide gracefully around in the water, or if you are a boy, you can parade around the pool like a character out of *Baywatch*. Similarly, you can perform gymnastics or go trampolining, aware that Person-U-Like is somewhere nearby, watching you. But make sure you know what you're doing, so that you don't go smack on your back (painful, dangerous and UNCOOL), or try to impress people by walking to the end of the diving-board, only to change your mind and crawl back along it, or end up doing a dramatic belly-flop.

✦ Sports gear, of course, is COOL. You can at least

SERIOUSLY COOL ATTITUDE TO SPORT

COOL, FOCUSED, ON THE DIVING-BOARD

UNCOOL, UNFOCUSED, ON THE DIVING-BOARD

LOOK the part, and show off your new trainers, etc. (Remember: you don't need to *say* anything about them. Just *wear* them, and let people notice. This is cool . . .)

COOL ATTITUDE TO WORK

The coolest attitude to work is to stay on top of it (I don't mean piling all your books/files, etc. on top of each other, and then perching dangerously on top of the teetering pile). Get it sorted as you go along. If you let it all pile up, so that you have a massive backlog, and it all begins to get on top of YOU, you will begin to lose your cool. Teachers will begin to lose *their* cool with you, and someone may even contact your parents, who will also lose their cool (Loss of Cool is highly infectious or even contagious, and prevention is better than cure). Ask yourself whether it is worth it.

KEEP ON TOP OF YOUR WORK

A Cool Attitude To Work means getting it sorted without being too obvious about it. DO NOT start bragging, 'Oh, I've done ALL my homework!' or, 'Wasn't that chapter we had to read on the effect of the Industrial Revolution on the lives of a family of box manufacturers in the North of England *fascinating*?' This sort of behaviour will make you seem like a SWOT, which is an UNCOOL thing to be. If you set aside a quiet hour or so every day for getting your work sorted, you can enjoy yourself with your friends and practise New Cool the rest of the time.

HOW TO BE A SHINING EXAMPLE OF NEW COOL WHILE AT SCHOOL

✦ DON'T sit right under the teacher's nose (unless the teacher's nose is excessively large and long, and reaches to the back of the class, in which case you can't help it).

✦ At the back of the class is the traditionally cool place to sit – but not if you're right under the bell, and you leap three metres into the air every time it rings. (If your nerves are this bad, you need to go back to the Basics of Cool, and practise your Relaxation Exercises. Breeeeeathe . . .)

IT IS UNCOOL TO SIT RIGHT UNDER THE TEACHER'S NOSE

✦ Keep your Cool in the Canteen. If you suffer from Queue Rage (you start sweating, grinding your teeth and generally losing your temper because there is a queue a mile long in front of you and you are right at the back of it, somewhere out beyond the goalposts on the rugby field – and you just can't WAIT to get to your turkey burger) it may be a better idea to take your own lunch to school. On the other hand, you could take the opportunity to relax and chat to friends as the queue moves slowly forward. Canteen Cool also involves finding a good place to sit, not too near to any teachers/swots/nerds/saddos, etc. and preferably in a position where Person-U-Like might actually notice you. Try to look cool as you eat your lunch, so avoid sticking chips up your nose or in your ears, flicking peas/ baked beans, or sneezing into your soup or slopping it everywhere, or stuffing whole sausages into your mouth or any other kind of anti-social mealtime behaviour. It is UNCOOL to be told off in front of everyone. Rebelling against School Rules is one thing. Being disgusting with your food is another. Cool Rules state that it is probably better to stick to School Rules rather than risk being made to look a complete fool in front of everyone (many teachers are experts at withering sarcasm – some of them have degrees in it – and you can definitely do without it).

✦ It is Cool to enjoy/be good at Art. It is not quite so cool to be wildly enthusiastic about Geography. Don't worry about it if you can't *help* enjoying Geography –

just keep it to yourself. (Wild enthusiasm about *anything* is probably best avoided if you want to be Cool. Quiet appreciation is fine.)

IF YOU WISH TO BE COOL, YOU SHOULD AVOID STICKING CHIPS UP YOUR NOSE

CHAPTER 5

Coolspeak

Sooner or later, of course, you will have to come out of your hiding place and face the world. If you practise the Basic Rules of Cool when things go wrong (relax, don't worry, don't try too hard, accept that things go wrong occasionally), your recovery rate should get faster, and you will be able to communicate calmly with friends again, without losing it.

NOTE: A time-honoured but still Cool way of dealing with anyone who is doing their best to wind you up is to ignore them, and quietly *change the subject*. Say, in a casual tone of voice, something like, 'Oh, by the way, have you seen that great new film about the woman who falls in love with an alien . . . ?'

COOL COMMUNICATION

One of the Basic Ingredients of Cool is a Cool Way of Talking. This involves using cool words and right-on

COOL GREETING

UNCOOL GREETING

expressions (Yeah!! Right on!!!). It also involves knowing WHEN to open your mouth, and when to keep it shut. It is frequently better, and cooler, to say NOTHING . . .

THE UNCOOL SCENE

A girl called Aisha and her friends Yasmin and Martin are trying to persuade Suni to go to the fair with them, but Suni knows that his mum wants to take him shopping that afternoon to get some essential items like trousers. Another reason is that he doesn't have any money, so he doesn't want to go . . .

AISHA: Come on, Suni – it'll be a laugh, I reckon!

SUNI: No, thanks. I have to go shopping with my mum.

YASMIN: WHAAT? You're joking. Can't you go another time?

SUNI: No, I have to go this afternoon. Mum says I have to.

MARTIN: Couldn't you just sneak off?

SHORT OF TROUSERS
(SHORT OF TROUSERS IS UNCOOL)

SUNI: NO! I couldn't do that! She'd be worried. Besides, Mum says I have a cold coming on, so I need to take it easy. Anyway, I need some trousers.

AISHA: What sort of trousers?

SUNI: Nice trousers. Mum chose them, and I've got to try them on so that she can see if they fit, and how much she needs to take them up.

AISHA: But there's a really BIG wheel and stuff! You MUST go on it. And the dodgems!

SUNI: I am afraid of heights. And last time I went on the dodgems, I was sick.

AISHA *(sighing)*: Oh, well. Suit yourself. Next time, then.

SUNI: Maybe. But I am a little short of money, as well as short of trousers, and it would be more sensible if I didn't go out.

So what is UNCOOL about the above scene? Well, just about everything, of course. But how CAN Suni get out of going to the fair with his friends (he really *doesn't* want to go) without seeming totally uncool? The difference between 'cool' and 'uncool' has a lot to do with the actual words used, and it has everything to do with what is said – and with what *isn't* said . . .

THE COOL SCENE

AISHA: Come on, Suni – it'll be a laugh, I reckon!

SUNI: Look – it's a real drag, I know – but I can't make it.

YASMIN: Why's that?

SUNI *(casually)*: Oh, I'm going shopping.

YASMIN: Cool! Getting anything special?

SUNI: Yeah. There's a pair of trousers I really want.

AISHA: But you'll miss the big wheel and everything.

SUNI: Sorry, guys. But I'll be spending all my cash on these trousers, see, and after that I'm going to be skint for a while.

MARTIN: Don't worry about it, mate – the dosh, I mean. You can hang out with us anyway. Any time.

SUNI: Cheers, mate. I appreciate it. See you, then!

The second scene is written in Coolspeak, which is a language that is continually being changed and updated (so apologies if some of these words and expressions are ALREADY out of date . . .).

COOLSPEAK RULES

Apart from the actual words, there are certain rules of Coolspeak which should be observed:

✦ NEVER begin a sentence with, 'Mum says that . . .' Instead of: 'Mum says that it is cold, so I must wear a warm coat,' you should say, 'It looks cold out there – I'll just grab my coat.'

✦ References to parents should be avoided, as far as is possible, except in the context of what a drag they are.

NOTE: If you are a member of an all-girl super-group, you can get away with singing a song called 'Mama – I love you!' But if you suddenly start singing this when you are out with your friends (especially if you are a boy), they are likely to pretend they are not with you.

✦ Speak for yourself. Make it sound as though you have an independent mind, and a life of your own. For example, 'I'm going shopping,' sounds better than 'I'm going shopping with Mum.'

✦ Avoid confessing to too many embarrassing weaknesses, such as being sick on the dodgems. It is probably better not to treat your friends to the more unsavoury details of your life (this may be funny, and very honest, but it is not COOL). You can confide in a close friend, but if you are too open and too honest (and talk too much?) with everyone, you expose yourself to the risk of teasing, taunting and being generally wound up by other people. Choose your friends carefully, and be careful *what* you say to *whom*. This is COOL.

✦ Avoid words like 'nice' and 'sensible'.

✦ Try to be decisive. Too much 'er . . . um . . . dunno . . .' is uncool.

✦ With good friends you don't need to try to be cool. You can gradually relax, and be yourself (and then you may well find out that it's cool, anyway. COOL – without trying!).

The coolest word of all, of course, is . . . COOL. Even just saying it makes you *feel* cool. Try it now. Say, 'COOOOOL!'

How do you feel? Pretty cool, huh?

WARNING: There is an exception to every rule, of course. The exception in this case (and in many other cases) is PARENTS. You should not *expect* the word 'cool' to work its magic on an irate father:

DAD: Your school report is dreadful! It is perfectly obvious that you have not been doing any work, just sitting and gawping at the TV. AND it says here that you were late for school every day, and on one occasion you didn't even turn up at all! Now – I want to know, WHAT'S GOING ON!?

YOU: Nothing's going on, Dad. It's cool.

DAD: NO! IT IS NOT COOL! And if you say *that* word one more time – just ONE more time, I . . . I . . . I . . . I . . . (*Dad has lost his cool to such an extent that he has got stuck, and no further words will come out. This is a relief. You should leave him alone, and give him time to chill out.*)

DAD HAS LOST HIS COOL TO SUCH AN EXTENT THAT HE HAS GOT STUCK

NOTE: Avoid telling your parents to chill out.

So now you think Cool, you look Cool, you act Cool, you are Cool. Cultivate a Cool Attitude. Keep a Cool head on your shoulders (where else would you keep it?).

WHEN COOL DESERTS YOU

So there you are – the embodiment of New Cool. You feel GOOD. You feel AMAZING. You ARE amazing . . . until . . . you bump into Person-U-Fancy-Like-Mad. SUDDENLY your Cool deserts you, *just* when you need it MOST. You revert to a grinning, stammering,

REMEMBER YOUR COOL WAY OF WALKING
(AND AVOID WALLS, DOOR-FRAMES, ETC.)

apologising, giggling idiot with hands that have become large, flappy things you don't know what to do with, and feet that you seem determined to trip over. Even if you manage your Cool Way of Walking, you walk into a wall, door-frame or bookcase.

As for your Cool Way of Talking, forget it. Literally – you have forgotten how to talk, and can think of nothing to say. (Yes – there are times when saying nothing is probably *not* cool, if it means that you stand there, with your jaw sagging, gazing helplessly at One-U-Adore, who has only stopped to ask you what the time is . . .)

WHY??! You ask yourself this question in anguish, over and over again. WHY? WHY? WHY? Have all your efforts to be COOL been in vain?

ANSWER: No, of course not. You have simply suffered a temporary setback and memory loss. You have forgotten the First Rule of Cool which is . . . RELAX. It is probably a good idea to return home and chill out for a while, and give yourself a chance to unwind, and think about what happened. (OK – you would really rather NOT think about what happened . . . but you can't *help* thinking about it . . . STOP! It is a question of thinking about it in the right way.)

RIGHT AND WRONG WAYS OF THINKING ABOUT EMBARRASSING ENCOUNTERS

Wrong Way Of Thinking About An Embarrassing Encounter With A Member Of The Opposite Sex: 'Oh, my god! I feel *so* STUPID! I AM STUPID! I hate myself! They must think I'm stupid! They must hate me! It's awful! My life is ruined!' etc., etc.

Right Way Of Thinking About An Embarrassing Encounter With A Member Of The Opposite Sex: 'Oh well, I don't suppose it was such a big deal. They've probably forgotten about it already. I'll see them again soon, so it doesn't matter. I'll be cool next time.'

Armed with this New Cool Attitude, you can face the possibility of seeing One-U-Adore (From Near or From Afar) again. Remember that they have doubts and insecurities too, even if they don't show them (and they DON'T walk into walls . . .). Set yourself the goal of putting *them* at their ease . . .

COOL AND UNCOOL CONVERSATION

THE COOL CONVERSATION SCENE

ONE-U-ADORE: Er, can you tell me the time?
YOU: Yeah. That's cool. It's five past three.
ONE-U-ADORE: Thanks.
YOU: By the way, how's things?

ONE-U-ADORE: Oh, er, fine! And you?

YOU: Fine. Fine . . . yes. Fine.

ONE-U-ADORE: That's great. See you, then!

YOU: Sure. Cool. See you!

It is not a scintillating conversation. But it IS a conversation. You have avoided trying too hard . . .

THE UNCOOL CONVERSATION SCENE

ONE-U-ADORE: Er, can you tell me the time?

YOU: Yeah. It's time you and I got it together. Right?

ONE-U-ADORE: Er . . . I only wanted to know what the time was. It doesn't matter . . .

YOU: Yes! You're so right! It doesn't matter! What IS time, anyway? Isn't it mad how we worry about what time it is? Does it *matter* whether it's five past three or ten to eleven?

ONE-U-ADORE: Well, yes, actually. Er, look – I've got to go!

YOU: Farewell, then! *Adieu, adieu! Au revoir!* Parting is such sweet sorrow. Alas.

This sort of showing off is usually off-putting to the other person (they don't know what to say, and they may think you are making fun of them). It is uncool. So take it easy. Don't worry if your conversation is limited to the 'Hi, how are you – fine,' variety, and never seems to get beyond that. Give it time. RELAX.

SILENCE IS COOL

If you suffer from chronic shortage of conversation, remember that a friendly and companionable silence is cool, as long as you are relaxed. If *you* relax, the chances are that the other person will relax, too. You could go for a walk (a slow, unhurried, Cool Walk), taking time out to observe the passing scene. It is cool to point out details such as beautiful light falling on a tree, or a squirrel running across the grass. Look OUT, rather than inwards towards the seething mass of insecurities inside you (not a pretty sight). Gradually, you will forget about being nervous, and the conversation may begin to flow naturally. If it doesn't, remember that it doesn't matter. You don't have to talk all the time – in fact, it is uncool to do so. Just be friendly – be yourself. Pretend to yourself that the person you're with is no one special, and so you don't really mind whether they like you or not (you are fooling yourself, of course, but it may help you to relax – it is a technique which takes a bit of practice). Always pause to consider that the other person may be feeling nervous or insecure, too. Cool is often a cover for shyness. Listening to music together is a good way of relaxing and maintaining your Cool. So is watching a video (something featuring the latest hot star, rather than a Disney film) or a TV programme ('The X-Files' rather than 'Blue Peter').

One occasion when the 'Silence is Cool' rule does not apply is when you are on the phone. You can run up an enormous phone bill if you spend hours on the phone saying nothing (a very pointless exercise indeed). In fact, the person on the other end is likely to become bored, and hang up. So before you pick up the receiver to make a call, you should consider in advance what you are going to say. In some ways, talking on the phone is easier than talking to someone face to face.

HOW TO BE COOL ON THE PHONE (PHONE COOL)

✦ Write down on a piece of paper all the things you want to say while you are on the phone. Try not to drop this piece of paper while you are talking, because the person on the other end will wonder what is going on: 'So would you like to come with me to the . . . aargh, I've

PHONE COOL

dropped it! . . . Hang on, sorry . . . Whoops, got it . . . There we are . . . er, what was I saying?' Be prepared for the dog/a little brother to run off with your piece of paper halfway through the conversation. If you can manage to hang on to your piece of paper, you can use it to doodle on. Doodling while you talk helps you to relax.

✦ Before picking up the receiver, clear your throat several times (you could even say, 'Testing . . . testing . . .' but make sure no one is around to hear you doing this), otherwise you may find that the moment Person-U-Like answers the phone, you lose your voice, or it dwindles into a strange, frog-like croak, which does not quite create the impression you were hoping for. (Or maybe it does – hoarse voices are said to be sexy, although you can easily take this too far.)

✦ Practise your super-sexy, seductive Phone Voice. It is difficult to convey exactly what this should sound like,

but if you speak slowly and clearly, in low and gentle tones, you are probably getting it right: 'Hi . . . iii'. *Enjoy* the words. Roll them around your tongue, and pour them like silk down the phone. If you are lucky, it will have the desired effect. If you are unlucky, the person on the other end of the phone will think you are completely mad. That is why it is wise to practise first. Try it out on a friend. You will probably fall about laughing.

IT MAY BE EASIER TO MAINTAIN YOUR PHONE COOL IF YOU DO NOT HAVE A LITTLE GROUP OF FRIENDS IN THE BACKGROUND ...

✦ On the subject of friends falling about laughing, you may find it easier to maintain your Phone Cool if you do NOT have a little group of friends in the background, shouting things over your shoulder (traditionally things like 'Hi, James! Laura's just calling to tell you she really LOVES you!' – designed to cause you maximum embarrassment) while you are making your call. You may *think* that you need their support and encouragement to make THAT call – but, to be honest, you are probably better off making a phonecall when you are on your own.

Cramming yourself and seven friends into a phonebox may be fun (and quite an achievement), but it is not cool.

✦ Some people think mobile phones are COOL. However, they aren't always that cool, if you're walking by heavy traffic, and Person-U-Like calls, and you find you can't hear what they're saying and vice versa, and you end up shouting at each other 'WHAT?' and 'SORRY?' Later on, you discover you misheard them when you miss your second date because you're waiting outside the wrong cinema. Beware of trappings which may seem cool but which are actually cool booby-traps.

✦ Another Basic Rule of Phone Cool is to avoid phoning someone and saying, 'Hi, it's ME!' It is not always easy to recognise someone's voice over the phone (some voices are more instantly recognisable than others). It will dent your confidence if the person on the other end says, 'Who? Who's that?' and you have to say, 'Er, it's me . . . you know, Laura . . . er, the girl at school with the red hair . . . the one you spoke to and asked the time . . . ?!?' It is better to state your identity as soon as the other person answers the phone: 'Hi, it's Laura.' If you wish to avoid the possibility of the other person saying, 'Which Laura?' (how many does he know? Fifty, at least . . .), you should state your surname, as well.

✦ Parents will do their best to cause serious damage to your Phone Cool. Your dad will storm around in the background, making clearly audible comments about the size of the phone bill. If someone phones YOU, your mum may get to the phone first and answer it, and you will find her saying something like, 'Oh, Jez . . . is it? Yes, I know who you are! Aisha's *always* talking about you. Here she is now, looking a little shy! Come on, Aisha – Jez wants to talk to you!' (She hisses the last bit in what is meant to be a whisper, but is so loud that the dog starts barking in the next room.) Try to make and receive phonecalls when parents are not around (although it is polite to at least ask your parent in advance if you may use the phone later). Ask your friends to call you at a time when you know your parents will be ELSEWHERE.

✦ Answering machines make most people feel uncool and sound unnatural. If you can remain cool while talking to an answering machine, you are a Cool Dude Indeed! (But have a go at leaving a *short* message, not your complete life history, with noises of siblings fighting and parents shouting in the background . . . Like most things, it will get easier if you practise.)

CHAPTER 6

Cool And The Opposite Sex

Having perfected your Phone Cool, how do you remain cool when you are actually with a member of the opposite sex?

UNCOOL BEHAVIOUR TO AVOID

✦ Talking too much in an effort to avoid awkward silences and cover up the fact that you are nervous. Try listening instead. Listen to the other person talking. Listen to more distant sounds: a door creaking, footsteps in the corridor, birds singing, the wind rustling the leaves, the roar of traffic. Feel the ground under your feet, the warm sun on your face (or rain down the back of your neck). Using your senses to connect with the world around you helps you to relax and stay cool, rather than concentrating on the sound of your own heart beating like a drum, or any other kind of inner turmoil.

✦ Jealousy. This is the uncoolest of emotions. It can make you act in a very uncool way.

THE UNCOOL SCENE NO. 1

Martin likes Pippi a lot, and they have been out together once. But Pippi is now going out with Martin's friend Jake. Martin and Jake have always been best mates, but suddenly Jake finds that Martin's attitude has changed.

JAKE: Yo, Martin! What's up?

MARTIN: What's it to you?

JAKE: I was only asking, mate!

MARTIN: Well, go and ask someone else! You're good at that. Asking someone else's girlfriend out, I mean.

JAKE: What? I don't know what you're on about.

MARTIN: No, you're too stupid. I don't know why she likes you.

JAKE: Ah! You're jealous.

MARTIN: NO I AM NOT JEALOUS! OK??!

JAKE: Cool it, mate.

MARTIN: NO I WILL NOT COOL IT . . .

Etc. etc. It is all very uncool. If you are jealous because Someone-U-Like is going out with Someone-U-No-Longer-Like, it is a doubly destructive emotion. It destroys your cool, for a start. If you let your jealousy show, it makes you vulnerable and uncool. You risk losing the friendship of Person-U-Like, and possibly also the friendship of the person they are now going out with. Since it is a situation you can do nothing to alter, why make it worse by driving your friends further away by a display of jealousy and anger? If you keep your cool, you should also keep your friends, and you make it more likely that Person-U-Like will turn to you if their current relationship doesn't work out. Being cool means being prepared to give things time, and accepting the fact that you can never be quite sure what is going to happen next – so it's best to relax, and watch things unfold . . . So if you feel jealous, DON'T let it show – just go with the flow . . .

✦ Avoid endlessly apologising. Even if you have lost your cool in front of everyone, there is no need to apologise to them (which is embarrassing). Everyone loses it occasionally. Just relax, regain your cool, and carry on as if nothing happened (this is the coolest way to go). It is uncool to apologise too much, as if apologising for your existence.

THE UNCOOL SCENE NO. 2

Suni and Laura are on their first date. They go to a film, and sit in one of the middle rows. The cinema is crowded. Suni has bought some popcorn, and offers the carton to

Laura. Laura takes it, but she is so nervous that she drops it, and popcorn goes everywhere.

LAURA: Oh, I'm really sorry!

SUNI: Don't worry – it doesn't matter.

LAURA: But it was so CLUMSY of me – I'm really, REALLY sorry!

SUNI: Look – it's OK. Don't worry.

LAURA: I'm not usually so clumsy. You must think I'm a complete idiot! I think I AM an idiot! I'm really stupid! I AM sorry!

SUNI: I know. I said it's OK. Stop apologising.

LAURA: Oh, I'm sorry.

SEVERAL PEOPLE IN THE ROW BEHIND: STOP APOLOGISING!

SUNI *(turning round)*: Sorry!

If you have upset someone, or had an argument, and there is a genuine need to apologise, simply say the word 'sorry' once, and leave it at that. The word 'sorry' works best when you say it (and mean it) just once. This sort of understated apology is cool. There is no need to say anything else. You have said it all with just one word, and maybe touched the person you are apologising to gently on the arm, and met their eyes. But once you start gabbling, 'Sorry sorry sorry!' and falling on your knees in front of the other person, possibly with

GROVELLING IS UNCOOL

your arms thrown around *their* knees, imploring them with tears and pleading cries to forgive you, you have entered the realms of SERIOUSLY UNCOOL.

REMEMBER: GROVELLING IS UNCOOL.

✦ The words 'thank you' should also be used in moderation by members of New Cool. They are words which go down extremely well with parents and with any other relation who has just given you something for your birthday or Christmas. They are also words which begins to sound decidedly uncool if you say them all the time to your boyfriend/girlfriend.

THE UNCOOL SCENE NO. 3

JEZ: Hi, Aisha! How's it going?

AISHA: Fine, thanks.

JEZ: How are your folks?

AISHA: They're fine, thank you.

JEZ: Here's the CD you wanted.

AISHA: Oh, THANK YOU! I can't wait to hear it. Thank you! Thank you! Thank you again.

JEZ: Er, don't mention it. I'm having a party soon. Want to come along?

AISHA: Oh, yes PLEASE! That would be REALLY COOL!!! Thank you SO MUCH!!! Thank you! Thank YOU!! THANK you! I can't thank you enough!

JEZ: I've noticed. Anyway, it's next Saturday.

AISHA: Cool. THANKS!!!

JEZ: Please stop thanking me.

AISHA: Sorry.

It is nice to say 'thank you', but it is uncool if you are too profuse in your thanks, or too eager to please.
NOTE: It is nice to be NICE – but it is uncool. 'Nice' is an uncool word . . . It will make more of an impression if you say 'thank you' once – and leave it at that.

THE COOL SCENE

JEZ: Hi, Aisha! How's things?

AISHA: I'm fine. How're you?

JEZ: Great, thanks. And how are your folks?

AISHA: They're fine.

JEZ: Here's the CD you wanted.

AISHA: Cool. Thanks. Can't wait to hear it.

JEZ: I'm having a party soon. Want to come along?

AISHA: Yeah. Great!

JEZ: I made this little box for you – it's got your initials on. It's for you.

AISHA: Oh, wow! It's great. Thanks, Jez!

NOTE: Don't over-use the word cool either. It's not cool to say it *all* the time. Coolspeak is largely a language of understatement. You say more by saying less. It is uncool to be over-enthusiastic, but it *is* cool to express appreciation when someone does something special, or says something special to you.

Don't overdo it – the thanks, the apologising, or any other kind of OTT behaviour. Just relax, go with the flow, and your Natural Cool will shine out (Inner Cool). If you are prepared to give it time, other members of New Cool are almost bound to warm to you, and you may even attract Someone Particularly Cool . . .

THE BOYFRIEND/GIRLFRIEND IN COOL

So now you have found your Partner In Cool (but remember that it is important to be Cool On Your Own, as well). You can strut your funky stuff together, and flash your Street Cred all over the place. But remember that it is easier to do this in some places than in others.

QUESTION: What do you do if your mum insists you have to look after your little sister, but you want to meet your Partner In Cool (PIC). (If their name was Nic, they would be PIC NIC – oh well, never mind . . .)

ANSWER: Take your little sister with you and meet as arranged. Introduce Little Sister as 'Trouble', 'the Pest' or a similar appropriate name. Don't act as if she isn't there/doesn't exist, because this will cause her to pester you even more, trying to get your attention, and she will make an even bigger nuisance of herself. The chances are that your PIC will think she is SWEET or CUTE (there is no accounting for taste).

Choose a place like the park to hang out, where there are big swings which you can sit on, and little swings and other things that will provide a distraction for Little Sister, so that she will leave you alone (apart from when she is on the swing, and yells 'Push me!' at you until you give in and push her . . .). In other words, act cool, and make the best of the situation. If you get all grumpy and keep complaining about what a drag it is, having your little sister with you, your PIC may begin to find YOU boring (boring is uncool . . .).

You need to be aware of things you can do and places you can go that will help you avoid the possibility of becoming bored/boring or uncool.

COOL THINGS TO DO TOGETHER

✦ Listen to music (a cool band or rock group. But if your dad insists on listening to The Greatest Hits of Buck's Fizz and dancing round the living-room to it, then it is probably time to leave the house . . .).

NOTE: Avoid putting on headphones to listen to music, and then singing along loudly.

✦ Watch a video (a Cool Video, not a video of your sixth birthday party, kindly brought out by your mum for public viewing – you ate too much Thomas the Tank Engine birthday cake, and threw up over a guest . . .).

✦ Watch TV (avoid watching wildlife programmes on the sex-life of the elephant in the company of parents, etc.).

✦ Go for a walk (anywhere that is not inhabited by teachers or parents).

✦ Go to a film or concert (a rock group, not the local brass band).

✦ Go to a fair (dodgems are cool and fun).

✦ Play computer games (but don't get stressed if you can't get beyond a certain level, and refuse to talk to the person you are with because they are better at it than you are. This is NOT cool. Have FUN . . .).

✦ If you can afford it, go to a café or round the shops (music stores are good. You don't have to spend any money).

✦ Go surfing (the sea or the Net . . .).

CHAPTER 7

Cool Creatures/ Uncool Creatures (Otherwise Known As Pets)

Pets. Aren't they wonderful? Some are positively life-enhancing, while others can destroy your Street Cred in an instant and cause you to lose your Cool completely (consider the dog which cocks its leg against the designer trouser-leg of Person-U-Fancy . . .). Nothing makes you look less cool than dragging an unwilling dog on the end of a lead, or, alternatively, being taken for a walk by an over-enthusiastic one. It is cool to take a cat for a walk on a lead through a busy shopping centre, but it has to be a particularly laid-back cat. Don't try it if your cat is at all neurotic (most are).

Before you rush off to the pet shop, you may wish to consider the following guide to the coolest and the uncoolest of pets.

COOL CREATURES

✦ **CATS** The cat is in a class of its own. It is the King or Queen (or it may have been neutered) of Cool. It puts eating and sleeping FIRST. You could try modelling yourself on your cat:

1 Pretend you don't care much about anything.
2 Find the most comfortable place to sit.
3 Adopt graceful, languid and totally relaxed attitudes and poses.

CATS ARE COOL

Avoid certain aspects of cat behaviour, such as:

1 Rubbing yourself round the legs of Person-U-Like (they will trip over you).
2 Eating too much grass (or anything else), and then throwing up on the carpet.
3 Scratching, fighting, hissing loudly and sharpening your nails on the furniture.
4 Singing loudly and tunelessly in the street at night,

when other people are trying to sleep. (Having a bucket of water thrown over you makes you look uncool.)

✦ **CHINCHILLAS** Very furry, very classy. You will have the added satisfaction of knowing you have saved them from being made into a coat. **WARNING**: Exotic pets are expensive and often hard to look after. It is certainly NOT cool to kill or neglect an animal . . .

✦ **SNAKES** Appearing with a large snake coiled round your waist will impress most people (and cause others to become hysterical).

✦ **RATS** Especially white ones, with red eyes.

✦ **LLAMAS** You need a large garden for these. They are difficult to housetrain, and tend to stand in front of the TV, blocking your view and refusing to move.

✦ **RABBITS** They have sex all the time, and nobody seems to mind!

✦ **LARGE, FIERCE-LOOKING DOGS** Some people consider these to be cool. They look menacing but, in reality, they are as soft as anything and they love YOU. (This is all very well until they try to kill someone's pet poodle in the park – see Uncool Creatures – and a nasty scene results, involving the poodle's owner, which leaves you feeling anything but cool.)

✦ **THE HORSE** A cool animal. But it is uncool to look like a horse (or sound like one, or smell like one). Try not to wear your jodhpurs ALL the time.

UNCOOL CREATURES

✦ **DOGS** Sorry, I know this is being a bit hard on Man's Best Friend, the Faithful Hound, the adored Family Pet, etc. etc. Dogs have many redeeming features, but they are seldom cool. They think it is cool to drool. Most suffer from an excess of boundless (or bounding) enthusiasm. They will race through prickly gorse bushes and foul stinking mud to retrieve a stick and bring it back to you. This is hardly cool behaviour. (But could you cope with a cool dog?)

DOGS ARE OVER-ENTHUSIASTIC (OVER-ENTHUSIASTIC IS NOT COOL – TRY TELLING THAT TO A DOG ...)

MOST UNCOOL DOG OF ALL: A miniature poodle (or anything which resembles a loo brush), especially if it has a topknot on its head, done up with a red ribbon, and goes by the name of Betty Lou. Your parent insists you take the stupid thing for walks (a real drag, literally, since Betty Lou keeps sitting down and refusing to move). You feel even more stupid if you are forced to use one of those extendable leads (and the dog wraps the lead round the legs of Person-U-Like, tripping them over).

PRINCIPAL REDEEMING FEATURE OF THE DOG: If it is a gentle creature which lays its head on the lap of Person-U-Like, and gazes up at them with melting brown eyes, you can say, 'He really LIKES you! He doesn't do that to everyone!' This type of dog can be an asset (unlike Betty Lou, who nips Person-U-Like on the ankle).

✦ **HAMSTERS** Yes, OK. I KNOW they're sweet. But that is not the point. It is not cool to be sweet. And it is hardly cool behaviour to run round and round in a little wheel all night. On the other hand, hamsters spend all day eating and sleeping, which is pretty cool. Hmm . . . perhaps hamsters have got it sussed, after all . . .

✦ **CHICKENS** Let's face it, there is nothing cool about a chicken. In order to be truly cool, you have at least to pretend to have some level of intelligence (although not too much – a university degree at the age of twelve is impressive, but not exactly cool). Chickens make stupid noises every time they open their beaks. If you have the same problem, and find yourself saying stupid things every time you open your mouth (although you are probably imagining that the problem is worse than it is), try saying nothing. You can adopt an air of mystery, as

THERE IS NOTHING COOL ABOUT A CHICKEN

if you know things that other people don't, but are keeping quiet about it. Chickens have never learned to do this.

✦ **FISH** The closest a fish comes to being cool is to be turned into fingers, frozen and stuffed in the deep freeze. 'Come and see my tank of tropical fish,' is a dubious chat-up line. There is something mesmerising about watching them, but also deeply boring after a while. Owning piranha fish may qualify as cool, until they eat your hand. On the whole, fish leave most people cold (not cool).

✦ **TORTOISES** Dead boring. In fact, it is difficult to tell whether they are actually dead, or just boring. They may be considered cool because they are relatively rare, and expensive to buy (not good reasons). A tortoise takes coolness to such extremes that for about six months of the year it is barely alive. This kind of coolness is to be avoided.

✦ **PARROTS** Funny birds, but not cool, UNLESS they have learnt to say rude words, and embarrass your parents by shrieking these words at the top of their voice when your least favourite neighbour is at the door.

Finally, it is important to recognise that certain aspects of animal behaviour are not that far removed from certain aspects of human behaviour. Recognising this fact and laughing about it with your mates or Person-U-Like is cool. If, however, you would prefer to do without the company of your moulting, smelly, over-enthusiastic dog when you have just bumped into Person-U-Like in the park, try hurling a stick with all your might so that the dog dashes off after it (be careful not to hit an unwary passer-by in the distance). You will now have a peaceful few minutes in which to chat without a panting, drooling, muddy thing shaking itself vigorously right next to you . . .

CHAPTER 8

Cool Conclusion

You should now be ready to join the ranks of New Cool (or maybe you are already a fully-fledged Cool Babe/Dude).

In order to re-assess your Cool Quota (CQ), answer 'yes' to any of the following statements which you agree with:

1 A Cool Hat is not cool in itself. It is the way you wear it that makes it cool. You need to KNOW you look good in it. A Cool Hat requires a Cool Head to wear it.
2 COOL is CONFIDENT.
3 Silence is Cool (except when you are on the phone). It is uncool to gabble and waffle, moan, whinge and complain, or just talk endlessly about yourself. . . (Try saying, 'I'm tired of talking about me, *you* talk about me!')
4 It is Cool to LISTEN . . .

5 Parents should be not seen and not heard (when you have company).
6 It is uncool to bite your nails, chew your hair, pick your nose, throw food about or scratch your backside in public.
7 It is UNCOOL to try too hard, or to want desperately to impress people.
8 Things don't always work out but . . . hey, that's life. I can still be cool.
9 Big, baggy clothes are cool. So is skin-tight gear. I wear what *I* feel good in . . .
10 Cats are COOL (cats only to answer this one, please).

If you answered 'yes' to all ten of these questions (although the last one doesn't really matter), you are a Supercool Babe/Dude. If you answered 'yes' to five or more of the above, your Cool Quota (CQ) is well above average. If you answered 'yes' to four or less, your CQ is still good, but you need to read this book again. If you disagreed with all the statements, then you DEFINITELY need to read this book again (and stop picking your nose and scratching your backside in public).

COOL CHECKLIST

1 Remember your Cool Way of Walking and your Cool Way of Talking.

COOL RULE:

Avoid hassle

(Or, if you can't avoid it — manage it)

2 Make the most of your appearance, but don't get uptight about it. RELAX.

3 Practise your Cool Smile in front of the mirror, and rehearse the cool things that you are going to say, such as, 'Hi!', 'Yo!', 'That's cool,' and other similar expressions. Remember that saying the word '*cool*' makes you feel cool. Practise with friends.

4 Think Cool. Act Cool. Look Cool. BE COOL.

Potential Source Of Hassle No. 1 :

PARENTS

Potential Source Of Hassle No. 2 :

FRIENDS

5 Once you have achieved maximum COOL, you should be aware of those who haven't quite managed it yet. It is not cool to sneer at them, and it is certainly UNCOOL to be MEAN. It would be much kinder to say nothing (simply lend them this book . . .).

REMEMBER: This whole book can probably be summed up in One Major Rule Of Cool, which is: AVOID HASSLE. Or, if you can't avoid it, manage it. There are many potential sources of hassle, such as parents,

Potential Source Of Hassle No. 3 :

SCHOOL

Potential Source Of Hassle No. 4 :

LUURRVE . . .

friends, school and LUURRVE – which is great, but, as the saying goes, the path of true love never was entirely hassle-free . . .

One thing is certain – life is full of hassle. You can't avoid it all, but you CAN avoid getting *hassled*. You CAN keep your COOL. You will then be ready to emerge into the Cool Light of Day (or the Cool Light of Night . . .).

Finally, if you want people to think you are REALLY cool next time you are out with friends, simply produce this book from your Cool Bag, or from one of the larger pockets in your Cool Trousers, and flash it around . . .

That's Cool